DISCARD

Making It

as a Stepparent

Claire Berman

Making It

as a Stepparent

NEW ROLES/NEW RULES

Updated Edition

PERENNIAL LIBRARY

Harper & Row, Publishers, New York
Grand Rapids, Philadelphia, St. Louis, San Francisco
London, Singapore, Sydney, Tokyo, Toronto

A hardcover edition of this book was originally published by
Doubleday & Company, Inc.
It is here reprinted by arrangement with the author.

First Perennial Library edition published 1986.

Library of Congress Cataloging-in-Publication Data

Berman, Claire.
    Making it as a stepparent.

    Bibliography: p.
    Includes index.
    1. Stepparents—United States. 2. Parenting—United States.
    3. Stepfamilies—United States—Psychological aspects. I. Title.
HQ759.92.B46   1986   306.8′74   85-45177
ISBN 0-06-097019-7 (pbk.)

98 RRD - H 20 19 18 17 16 15

This book is for Hazel and Samuel Berman
and for Ruth Von Dohlen (a.k.a. Rufus)
for taking steps that have enriched my family

Contents

Acknowledgments

For their contributions to this book, I am greatly indebted to the many women, men, and children who welcomed me into the private worlds of their families and who shared their experiences that others might learn. It is a pleasure to relive the good times of one's life; many stepfamily members who were interviewed clearly enjoyed the opportunity to do so. But there were also many who were asked to recall incidents of conflict and moments that had caused them pain. It was not comfortable for them to speak of the issues they had faced, and yet they did not flinch from disclosure. To them, I am especially grateful. To encourage candor, I promised anonymity. Hence, I cannot name the families, but I hope they will accept my gratitude and my respect.

To James D. Meltzer, Ph.D., I offer thanks for the generosity with which he shared his knowledge and for his advice, encouragement, and friendship.

Many other mental health professionals were generous with their time and information. Their contributions are cited throughout this work.

To Eli Kramer, Hazel Schizer, and Aryeh Friedman, able attorneys all, goes my appreciation for their help in guiding me through the maze of legal issues, for making the complex clear.

Naomi Bernstein was good-natured about looking up sources and statistics.

It was chance that led me to Marcia Amsterdam. Thus I was

able to benefit from her creative inspiration and her interest in this project.

To Karen Van Westering, a talented editor, goes appreciation for her recognition that the challenge of the stepfamily had to be addressed. Throughout the research and writing of this book, she offered helpful suggestions and, even more important, encouragement when it was needed.

They also serve who take the children away on weekends. For this, and for support given in innumerable ways, I am grateful to my husband, Noel Berman. Kind thoughts are extended as well to Eric, Mitchell, and Orin Berman, on general principles.

—C.B.

Preface to the Updated Edition

"Where were you ten years ago when I needed help?" wrote a reader of the original edition of this book.

"I felt as if you had interviewed me, although we have never met," I heard from another.

Week after week, my mail contained letters from men and women across the country who were grateful to learn that their feelings and experiences as members of remarried families were *normal*. And to read about how others coped with the special challenges of stepfamily living. Clearly, the book had met a need.

That need remains, even though the past several years have seen greater openness on the subject of stepfamilies. The media have taken even more enthusiastically to the topic, exploring the various aspects of remarried life. It's an issue frequently aired on radio and television talk shows; the feature pages of newspapers and magazines are likewise filled with tales of how "blended families" manage their lives.

I have come to dislike that term. To refer to a remarried family as "blended" perpetuates the myth that the differences between second- and first-wed families will blur and a unit strongly resembled the nuclear family will emerge. Families that fail to blend—and why should they obscure their different histories, experiences, and allegiances?—often feel that they have failed. Instead, I believe that members of stepfamilies (and *that* is the term I prefer) should recognize the ways in which their situation is unique from the first-wed family—not better, not worse, but different. Accepting the differences, stepfamily members must work to create a satisfying lifestyle. It can and is being done.

Feelings that began to form during the writing of this book have been strengthened during the years since its publication. I was invited to speak before a variety of groups across the country—groups made up of divorced persons, remarried individuals, educators and guidance counselors, lawyers and judges, professionals in the field of mental health, religious leaders to whom many turn for counsel. I became even more involved in the subject of remarriage, eventually serving, in 1984, as president of the Stepfamily Association of America.

It was an enriching and enlightening experience. Enriching because of the many wonderful people I met who are directing their energies to the creation of successful families (albeit that effort is seldom easy). Enlightening because as I lectured I learned. And what I learned is that the need remains for information, education, and sharing about what it is like to live in a stepfamily. I am, therefore, grateful to Barbara Seaman for directing me to Janet Goldstein, editor at Harper & Row, and to Janet for recognizing that the story of how to "make it" as a stepparent is one that bears retelling.

"Twice upon a time," this story begins. . . .

Making It

as a Stepparent

Introduction

"I wasn't seeking to become a mother, but there was no choice. I was deeply, romantically involved with a man and I knew his children came as part of the package. If I wanted him, I'd have to take them. And I wanted him. So we were married. It didn't take long before I discovered the package was ticking and likely to explode."

The speaker, Susan Graham, is a lively young woman who has just celebrated her thirtieth birthday. This is her first marriage. Eric Graham, her husband, is forty-one. His three daughters are aged fourteen, ten, and seven. The girls alternate weekly living arrangements, one week in Eric and Susan's apartment and the next in the house Eric once shared with their mother. Susan is their stepmother.

She has found it a difficult role.

But not at first. At first she was determined to be the best mother the children had. (She conveniently refused to acknowledge that "other woman," the one the girls were born to and with whom they lived at least half the time.) And Eric encouraged her in this fantasy. Susan sensed, correctly, his wish that she be a better mother than his first wife. Their neighbors and friends gave the family rave reviews: "wonderful mother" . . . "lucky children." (People who live with other people's children are fair game for scrutiny by well-meaning commentators.)

What then was wrong with this package? For one thing, the children neither wanted nor *needed* another woman cast in the role of mother. For another, Susan found that the lines she was assigned were all wrong for her character. She found herself under great pressure to succeed, to measure up—but to what standard? There were no cues to guide her. All her ideas about family were based on traditional concepts of the nuclear, once-wed family unit. This was the model she was supposed to follow. And so, Susan, once a dedicated career woman, now threw herself with equal fervor into the mothering role. She cooked, she cleaned, she played Scrabble, she baked brownies. Nobody said thank you.

For a time, she submerged her resentment.

Susan continued to struggle with the part of fairy godmother because she feared taking on the contrasting role, that of the classic wicked stepmother. For the same reason, she expressed her doubts and her feelings to no one, lest others judge her as harshly as she was coming to judge herself.

The situation became very tense, with Susan and Eric arguing about all sorts of little things because they were afraid to face up to the real issue: Susan did *not* love the girls.

She'd been so busy trying to play Supermom, she hadn't taken the time to find out if she *liked* her stepdaughters. She recalls clearly the day she confronted Eric with this reality. It was right after they'd been engaged in a whale of a fight. Susan has forgotten the ostensible cause of that argument, but she does recall that the real reason suddenly became clear. "I have a relationship with you . . . and your daughters have a relationship with you," she told her husband. "I am *not* their mother. The girls and I will have to work out our relationships, recognizing that we have ties to one another through you, and we'll just have to see what happens."

Although it was a painful admission to make (and even more distressing a confession for Eric to hear), Susan found it also was a liberating declaration, one that freed the members of the family to explore who they were and how they felt about one another. *The evolution of these new relationships, for which no realistic role models currently exist, is the major challenge that must be met by all who are involved in the stepfamily experience.*

Susan Graham asked to be interviewed for this book, as did so many other men and women who learned of the project, because she strongly believes that all the members of the Graham family would have been spared a great deal of pain if *someone* had come forward and spoken candidly to them about the realities and the expectations of families in which one or both partners must learn to live with children from a previous marriage, children who are not their own.

It should be noted that stepparents "live" with the reality of the children even if they do not physically reside in the same home with them. Listen to one Atlanta-based woman whose son had left her home and gone East to live with his father while her (second) husband's son and daughter made their home in Minneapolis with *their* mother: "The kids are always there between us. I can honestly say we never have a moment without them. For instance, Howard [her second husband] and I just had a fight—a rather typical one, and I don't know any remarried people with children who don't have a similar problem. Howard analyzes what's wrong with my son, which causes me pain, or he tells me that his daughter wants to get to know *me* better, which I see as a challenge, a shorthand declaration that I'm not trying hard enough to get her to like me. And I respond, 'Well, she knows where I am!'

"I'm angry with Howard's daughter right now because, on her last visit, I bought her a blouse she'd particularly admired, and she gave me a big thank you and then pointedly left it behind when she went home. She knew that would hurt me, and she was right. It did. But the important point is that Howard and I fought about all of this at breakfast *this morning,* and not one of the children has been to see us for three weeks!"

No two stories of families living in step situations are alike, which holds true for any family when compared with another, but some common concerns do emerge in conversations with participants in combined families, whether those families have been created following divorce or the death of a parent. *Most important is the recognition that stepparenting is different from primary parenting.* It can be just as satisfying, it can be a reciprocally loving and caring relationship between parent and child, and it can provide some very good moments when it works, but it is different.

"For better or worse," said a father who is now in his second marriage, "stepparenting is self-conscious parenting." He added emphatically, "You're damned if you do, and damned if you don't."

It is also analytical parenting and differs from natural parenting in that there is much less spontaneity about it. This is true for
the stepchild as well. One stepdaughter, now grown up, married,
and herself a mother, likened the caution of a step relationship to
an in-law one: "You react spontaneously to a parent," she explained, "and no matter how angry you become or how intem-
perate your speech, most of what is said in anger is forgotten. In
dealing with a stepparent, you are conscious of your tone and
your testimony—much as you'd be with your mother-in-law.
You're always aware of the relationship."

Those involved in step do a good deal of thinking about who
said what or did what to whom, and what everyone involved
meant by everything he or she did. Then the world at large scruti-
nizes the stepfamily's situation as well. Would the neighbors and
friends who reviewed Susan Graham's "performance" have felt as
free to criticize her handling of children who were born to her?
Most certainly not.

And don't think the stepparent is unaware of this. A forty-year-
old stockbroker recalls having been a skinny little kid who was
constantly being admonished by his stepmother to eat. "Eat," she
goaded, "or else everybody will think I'm a wicked stepmother."
In many stepfamilies, a concern for what "everybody will think"
hovers over the performance of those who become parents
through marriage.

Nor is this Greek chorus of helpful onlookers beneficial to the
children. That such benign intervention can have a negative effect
was stressed by a woman who spoke of her second marriage—this
one to a prominent doctor whom she met several years after her
first husband, a professor, had walked out on her and the couple's
two sons and gone off with one of his students. Following the
woman's remarriage, the doctor was quickly accepted in the small
community, both because of his own warm manner and because
relatives and friends of the abandoned family were genuinely
pleased to see the home restructured so constructively.

At home, however, the brothers missed few opportunities to
make their mother's new husband feel like an intruder in their
lives. Said their mother, "Too many other people were telling my
sons how lucky they were to have a new father, what a wonderful
man he was, and more of that sort of thing, but the boys had

never been given an opportunity to reach that decision for themselves."

You will find a somewhat greater number of women than men speaking through the pages of this book. Stepmotherhood remains the more challenging role (some noteworthy movement toward a more equal situation notwithstanding), largely because society still regards the woman as the nurturing parent and judges the adjustment of the family by how well or how poorly the substitute female parent seems to be faring. Stepmothers seemed to welcome the chance to communicate honestly the stress they found in their situation, the feeling that their efforts were undervalued in an ofttimes thankless job. . . .

In the light-splashed breakfast room of a home in the suburbs of Washington, D.C., a middle-aged woman and man discuss their blended family. Living at home is the woman's twelve-year-old daughter, the two older children having grown up and moved out, and the man's eighteen-year-old son, who seems to his father and stepmother to exist only to quarrel. He is a vegetarian and a critic of family meals and mores.

"The role of the stepmother is the most difficult of all," this woman explained, "because you can't ever just *be*. You're constantly being tested—by the children, the neighbors, your husband, the relatives, old friends who knew the children's parents in their first marriage, and by yourself. I feel I have to be a supermother to make it."

If there are echoes of Susan Graham here, it is no coincidence, for I heard this mentioned time and again: the pressure to be an ideal parent under conditions that are far from perfect. The Washington matron was not a supermother, by her own admission and her husband's concurring assessment—but the family *is* making it.

How are they doing it? How do families living in step order their daily lives? How do they meet the challenges of adjustment? How do they merge two different life styles, two or more sets of rules? How do they mete out discipline to *all* the children: his, hers and, in many situations, theirs? How do they decide where to establish their reconstituted home: "your place or mine?" How do they find privacy in the midst of confusion? How do they plan the special occasions of life, the weddings, bar mitzvahs, confirmations, graduations, the Thanksgiving, Christmas, and New Year's celebrations?

These are some of many questions I have asked of hundreds of remarried men and women across the country, and of their children, and of those mental health professionals who have interested themselves in many of these issues as helpers or researchers. The answers make up the material of this book. The stories, in which names and clearly identifying descriptions of persons who shared their private worlds with me have been changed unless otherwise authorized, are presented as the men and women related them.

I have not set out to write a how-to book. Each husband, wife, child, former mate, present lover, former in-law, grandparent, and stepgrandparent must work out "how to" create a satisfying personal and communal life within the framework of his or her own style and family situation. But I believe it will be helpful for those who struggle with the challenges of combining families to learn how others are coping and groping their ways in this wilderness, to profit from the accounts of good and bad experiences, and perhaps of greater importance, to find that difficulties they experience in their home are not unique to their situation, that they are not alone.

How could they be? It doesn't take a social scientist to observe that American family life has been undergoing great change. The divorce rate in the United States far exceeds that of any other nation. Between 1965 and 1982, the country's divorce rate doubled. to 5.0 per 1,000 population. In 1983, there were 11,589,000 currently divorced persons in the country. Projections done by the National Center for Health Statistics showed that, if current rates continue, almost 50 per cent of all marriages that took place in the 1970s will end in divorce.

The soaring divorce rate, however, does not reflect a general dissatisfaction with the institution of marriage. Some 73 per cent of divorced men and 66 per cent of divorced women will remarry, on an average of three years after the dissolution of the first marriage. In 1978, about 10.2 per cent of an estimated 63.2 million children under eighteen were living with two parents, one of whom was their stepparent. Close to five out of every six of these children had one or both current parents who had been divorced, and the remainder had parents who had been widowed but not divorced. Added to these figures are a large number of children in households in which their parents is "living in" with a member of the opposite sex in a familylike setting that presents the same problems of the stepfamily, albeit the terms for parent substitutes are not used.

While living with other people's children no longer is a unique experience, those who are doing it perceive (correctly) that it still is not sanctioned by a great segment of society. Recognition of stepfamilies, many believe, must be followed by a redefinition of roles and by new vocabulary to describe new relationships.

"With the rising rate of divorce and remarriage, society must come to terms with the fact that the new families so formed cannot be nuclear units, but are complex extended families linked by the marriage-divorce-remarriage chain," wrote Canadian lawyer Alastair Bissett-Johnson, a member of the McGill University Faculty of Law, Montreal.

The contemporary extended family is a multiple (rather than a unit) of interrelated, intricately connected individuals whose diverse relationships are apparent in a brief listing of some modern-day role assignments. Let's take a look at some kinship vocabulary: biological or natural parent, custodial parent, nonresident parent, stepparent, stepchild, stepsibling, half-sibling, father's wife's children, mother's husband, father's wife, grandmother, stepgrandmother, father's wife's mother, mother's husband's brother . . . and on it goes. The possibilities boggle the mind of anyone who pauses to contemplate them.

Those who are studying the stepfamily find the vocabulary wanting. "The English kinship terms for stepparents and stepsiblings are singularly inadequate," wrote Paul Bohannan in *Divorce and After*. "In the days before the divorce rate soared and before the death rate was lowered, the term 'stepmother' or 'stepfather' referred to new people in the household who substituted for the 'real' parents who were dead. . . . Today, the stepparent is less often a substitute parent than he is an added parent."

Bohannan also uses the term "coparental divorce" because both parties, although divorced from one another, *remain* parents to the child.

Among the professionals who have focused their attention on combined families, Rutgers sociologist Lucile Duberman also points to the need for role redefinition. In her book on *The Reconstituted Family* (note again the introduction of new terminology), Duberman points out: "In primary families, within which parents and children have known each other all of the children's lives, there is a unity which evolves slowly, without deliberation. This, however, is manifestly impossible in families of remarriage, where the members have separate histories and memories, and different concepts of roles, values, norms, and goals. Solidarity, the concept members of a family have of themselves as one functioning unit, must be carefully cultivated if it is to be achieved. Status, duties, and privileges must be redefined in the context of the new family."

Following years of being ignored, stepfamilies are coming into the spotlight. Newspaper columns fill feature space with reports of this trend. The doings of stepfamilies, as they search for rituals meaningful to their new life styles, are looked upon as the latest fad, a bit of contemporary exotica. Witness this report of a wedding:

> The maid of honor wore a white pinafore. The best man and the usher were attired in matching blue blazers and checked pants. After the wedding, everybody went to the reception at the country club where the maid of honor, the best man, and the usher were seen catching frogs down by the pond.

Thus began an account of an actual wedding reported in the pages of *The New York Times*. The maid of honor was eleven, the best man, thirteen, and the usher, eight. All three were described as "model attendants at their mother's second marriage." Later that year, the children attended their father at *his* second marriage. "I'm getting the hang of it now," remarked the thirteen-year-old.

Such amusing accounts do much to minimize a realization of the complexity of merging sequential families.

Stepparents appear on television talk shows, are the subjects of documentary reports, write books about their own experiences, publish newsletters, and establish organizations designed to educate and to provide self-help to the members.

The importance of all these efforts was underscored by a stepparent-panelist at a one-day group session held in Garden City, Long Island. "When you find yourself having problems in a step relationship," the speaker explained, "you also quickly discover you have no one to turn to. You can't go to your friends because they will judge you. And you don't want to be seen as washing your dirty linen in public. You can't turn to your parents, because they haven't been there, and they don't know how to advise you. If they hear too many complaints, their response is likely to be, 'Who told you to get divorced [or remarried] in the first place!' "

In support groups, which generally are guided by trained counselors, members of families who live in step are encouraged to express their feelings about one another, about their mutual and individual children, about those *other* parents—the ever-present ghosts who stalk the days and nights of the restructured family's new life. Many who speak up in group do so haltingly. For them, it is the first time they have been able to bring their feelings out into the open. Others are expressive, expansive. In groups, they can speak freely about topics that are taboo in the outside world. Here they learn they can share. It is a liberating experience. Here, too, many are taught *how* to communicate, how to make sharing an ongoing experience.

Nor do the problems of living in step cease when the children no longer live in the home. Divorce occurs at every age. No longer is it viewed as a response to a seven-year itch. The headlines tell the story: *Governor Nelson Rockefeller and his wife Mary divorce after twenty-two years of marriage, five children.* Divorce is no longer seen as the kiss of death to a political career; Rockefeller remarried and was appointed Vice-President of the United States. . . . In the first divorce granted to an immediate member of the British royal family since 1540, when Henry VIII divorced Anne of Cleves, England's Princess Margaret is granted a divorce from Lord Snowdon after eighteen years, two children. Lord Snowdon remarries.

Mature men and women seek to build new lives; they remarry and discover there are problems in the step situation that they had not been prepared to meet. The more desperate the desire for a new beginning, the greater is the remarried person's refusal to look at the roadblocks ahead.

Honesty is a part of the process. It is not a solution. Statistics underscore the difficulties of the situation. It has been estimated that 57 per cent of all remarriages will end in redivorce. The most frequently cited reasons for the breakup of second marriages are *children* and *money,* in that order. Nor are these necessarily two separate issues. Child care expenses (especially where there are offspring from more than one marriage) take a major bite out of any family's budget. The problems have been stated. The solutions to them are a continuing challenge.

A final thought: As the trees too often obscure the forest, so does a long list of concerns and considerations keep many from seeing the pleasures to be found when a group of strangers learn to live with and to love one another.

Countless boys and girls are finding their lives broadened and enriched by the presence of four caring parents and by an untold number of new relatives and friends. They are enjoying the opportunity to experience a variety of life styles and to select from each that which seems to suit them best.

During the course of researching this book, I spoke with many stepparents and stepchildren who expressed great satisfaction with the new people who came into their lives. Many broken homes have been made whole by the process of remarriage and recommitment and renewal. In their reconstructed families, many men, women, and children have discovered friendship. In commitment, some have been helped to find themselves.

Two myths must be shattered: that of the evil stepparent (be it Cinderella's wicked stepmother or, to a lesser degree, Hamlet's unfeeling stepfather) and the myth of instant love, which places unrealistic demands on *all* members of the blended family. Inevitably, overexpectation results in disappointment. Between the two opposing myths lies reality. The recognition of reality is, I believe, the most important step toward the building of a successful second family. The ideal—that picture of One Big Happy Family— may not be attained, not in stepfamilies nor (one begins to suspect) in original, first-wed, intact families.

Perhaps the challenge is to create one moderately sized, reasonably content kind of family. Perhaps that is the goal that *can* be achieved.

1

Instant Parent

If Audrey Kendall's real name were made known, it would be recognized as belonging to a celebrated decorator, a career woman whose talent and drive have brought her notable success. Two years ago, at the age of thirty-eight, Audrey was married to interior designer John Miles, forty-six. It was her first marriage, his third.

John brought with him two children of his second marriage, Jessie, eleven, and John, Jr., eight, who is called Jed by his family. John had been granted custody of the children as part of a divorce settlement reached with their mother three years earlier.

Audrey brought with *her* a love for John and an eagerness to become a parent. "I was approaching forty," she said, "and I had never been married. I think I'd always wanted to be a mother. To be honest, part of the appeal of marriage to John was that children were included in the offer."

So it was that Audrey Kendall became an "instant parent," a term used here to describe a woman or man who takes on a parenting role (full or part time) for the first time by marrying a spouse who has children.

Said Audrey, "I was totally unprepared for what followed."

Although she had intellectually, even eagerly, accepted the entrance of children into her well-ordered life, the romantic side of Audrey had been harboring "a honeymoon fantasy, of John and I just being a couple." Reality presented a different picture. "One moment I was single," Audrey said, "and the next moment I'd become a family!"

It was not a gentle transition.

"There were so many practical concerns that had to be handled right away—schools, visits to the orthodontist, pediatrician, music teacher, to name just a few," she continued, "romance became the *least* of my considerations. At least, that's what I kept telling myself. And the children really were so nice and so quickly accepting of me, I began to hate myself as I found I was growing to resent them . . . and, by extension, their father."

Audrey tried to suppress her feelings. After all, hadn't John been honest with her from the beginning? Hadn't he been clear in telling her that theirs would be a love-me-love-my-children marriage? And hadn't *she* been the one who'd pressed more strongly for institutionalizing the relationship?

What was wrong with her now?

Audrey was going through a typical critical period of instant parenthood, one that may be as predictable as childhood's terrible twos. It is a crisis that comes about when premarital fantasy is replaced by postmarital fact.

Dr. Richard A. Gardner, associate clinical professor of Child Psychiatry at Columbia University's College of Physicians and Surgeons, addressed this phenomenon in his practical guide, *The Parents' Book About Divorce*. Dr. Gardner wrote,

> A woman with no children of her own, when involved with a man with children whom she wishes to marry, may entertain unrealistic fantasies about how wonderful life will be with him and his children. . . . After marriage, and the lessening of romantic euphoria . . . the bride may become oppressed with the new burden she has taken on. Other women ease into the role of motherhood and gradually become accustomed to its frustrations. Having it thrust upon her cannot but produce feelings of being trapped and overwhelmed.

The Rescue Fantasy

At the same time, the natural parent must confront a reality that is equally unsettling. Psychologist James Meltzer, who directs an ongoing study of stepparenting roles at New York's William

Alanson White Institute of Psychiatry, Psychology and Psycho-analysis, sees the natural parent as one who harbors a rescue fan-tasy: the new parent will join our family and *all* our problems will be solved. . . . Johnny will do better in school; Mary will stay at home and stop fooling around . . . and so on.

"It's an enormous burden for the stepparent," says Dr. Meltzer, "an expectation nobody can live up to." But it takes time and travail before that realization sinks in.

The rescue fantasy is not limited to the caretaking parent. It is often indulged in by the stepparent who comes upon a family in chaos and decides to become the hero who will set matters right. Typically, this role is volunteered for by a man who has had no previous experience as a parent. Sociologist Gerda L. Schulman has described him as "someone who in his early years was an 'anti-family' man . . . but later settled down and wanted to make up for the loss of time, unconsciously hoping for respectability and stability."

This instant father can be very authoritarian. Perhaps because we have been raised to view the male as an authority figure, his assertiveness is regarded more favorably by the wife and, ulti-mately, the children he has joined than is similar strong control when exercised by a woman who takes on the challenge of instant parenthood. Many men find great satisfaction in acting out the rescue fantasy.

Buddy was a drifter, an ex-marine and sometime house painter who rented a room in a boardinghouse outside of San Francisco while he made up his mind about whether to re-enlist. On the floor directly above his room (as he discovered when he went up to complain about the noise) lived Jan and her two young chil-dren. The family was demoralized by years of having lived on-again off-again with a drug-dependent father.

Buddy befriended the family. He helped Jan with her budget, baby-sat for the children while Jan attended night school, and found he liked the responsibility, liked having the children look up to him. Buddy took a job as a stock clerk in a local super-market—"for the time being"—and recently was named assistant manager. He also married Jan.

"Being a stepfather to children who have never learned to trust a man, setting limits and at the same time getting the kids to like me, has been much harder than I realized," said Buddy. "But the change has been good for me. The knowledge of how much I was needed, especially by the children, made me settle down and take a steady job for the first time in my life. When I see how well the kids are doing, at home and in school, I know it's because of me, and that gives me a lot more respect for myself. I'd say that being a stepfather is well worth the effort."

Rescue fantasies aren't necessarily bad.

A Matter of Privacy

Typically, the instant parent is frustrated by an immediate loss of privacy.

"In any brand-new marriage, there ought to be a cocoon period when the marriage grows without intrusion. The touching time of a new relationship generally hasn't an audience. In step, it does." The speaker, Marie Shukaitis, is a family therapist who with Joseph Chuman, leader of the Ethical Culture Society of Bergen County, New Jersey, organized and directs stepparenting groups at the Society. Both professionals are instant parents.

The lack of privacy quickly becomes an issue with all couples where children are present at the start of the marriage. It is felt most keenly by first marrieds (and even more so by first marrieds who were only children) who are unaccustomed to the pervasiveness, the ongoing nature of the presence of children. It is the first-time parent who has the greatest adjustment to make.

"When I married and moved in with Hillary," said Mike, a thirty-four-year-old television cameraman, "her son Scott, who was then three, would climb out of his bed and curl up on the floor outside the door to our bedroom. He'd make little whimpering noises. Night after night. It didn't seem to bother Hillary as much as it did me. I felt I was an intruder, as though the child was outside trying to protect his mother. I began to feel self-conscious about touching his mother, with the boy out there. Hillary would get up, comfort Scott, walk him back to his bedroom . . . and the next night he'd be back, stationed outside our door. Finally, one night, I became angry. I got up, walked out, gave Scott one swat, and *ordered* him to bed. Once I stopped courting the boy, our relationship improved."

There's an interesting postscript to this story. Three years ago, Mike and Hillary had a child. As fate would have it, this little girl, too, is a night visitor. She often wanders into her parents' room after they have gone to bed. Mike reassures the child, carries her back into her own bedroom. He feels none of the tension that was brought on by his stepson's midnight forays. A lack of privacy is more keenly felt in step, especially by the adult who has never learned to live with children.

Audrey Kendall, whom we met earlier, also spoke of the matter of privacy. "I don't only mean privacy in bedroom terms," she said. "Ever since my marriage, I find there is *nothing* I can do without an audience.

"As a single woman who lived alone," she explained, "I liked to take my time before an evening out. There was almost a ritual to my preparations, and I found it pleasant. I'd come home from a busy day at work, and I'd shower. Then I'd pour myself a glass of wine or sherry, blow my hair dry, do my make-up, and generally work at getting rid of the tensions of the day. *Now,* I can't even apply make-up without one of the children coming into the dressing room and talking to me all the while. Jed wants to tell me about something that went on at school during the day. . . . Jessie just likes to watch me put on my eyeshadow. I've got the whole procedure down to ten minutes, and how I wish they could be ten private minutes, but they're not. And, yes, I feel a bit unhappy about that."

Joseph Chuman, leader of the Bergen County Ethical Culture Society (and co-leader of the stepparenting group, with Marie Shukaitis), was a young bachelor who, at twenty-six, moved in with Linda, a woman whose six children ranged in age from five to twelve and a half. Four years later, Chuman commented with classic understatement, "My transition from singlehood to parenthood hasn't been all calm."

Although Chuman expected life with Linda to be somewhat chaotic ("My relationship with Linda's children was simultaneous with my relationship with her," he recalls), he has been interested to observe how differently he and Linda respond to the intrusiveness of the children in their lives.

Says Chuman, "Linda is much more tolerant of children wandering into our room, flopping on our bed, and watching televi-

sion, going through our closets—even mine—when they're looking for something. I don't like that, and I tell them so very firmly.
I need space and time for me. Of course, the kids see these edicts
as deprivation, as a loss of something they had (in this case, the
run of the house before I came along) rather than an affirmation
of my need for space. Nevertheless, I think you must have the
strength to say, 'This may seem like deprivation, but these are my
needs.' "

What of the needs of the natural parent? Suppose that parent to
be a male. The children may be his, but the natural parent is feeling terribly unnatural in the new family unit. He too is working at
new relationships. He too would like time alone with his spouse.
But he is supposed to be patient and understanding. After all,
these are his children. Where the instant parent is expected to
show instant love, the natural parent must be instantly grateful.

What has life been like for John Miles, who is the natural parent in his restructured family?

"In a strange way," said John, "the lack of privacy continues to
bother me more than it does Audrey. In my previous marriage, I
was the Monopoly Daddy. I'd come home from the office, go into
the den and read the paper, join the family at dinner, and play a
game of Monopoly with the children before their bedtime. Now,
because I'm the biological parent in this home and because I've a
working wife who is *not* the children's mother, I feel I have to be
more involved with the nitty-gritty of child care, that I can't leave
it all to Audrey.

"By the time I've finished helping Jessie with her homework, I
find that Audrey's involved in a game with Jed. Then the dishes
have to be done. If there's time for conversation after that, whatever we talk about seems to have something to do with the children. I've found myself becoming petulant. I *need* time for myself
and I *want* some time with Audrey. I seem unable to achieve either."

Jealousy

"The fact is," John Miles continues, "I'm jealous of the time
Audrey spends with the kids. Although I wanted her to get close
to my children, I have to admit I'm jealous when it seems she's
succeeded too well. Let me show you what I mean . . . and if it

sounds petty, you'll see how unreasonable I've become: after she's said good night and gone to bed, Jessie will always call to Audrey for a glass of water. She doesn't want *me* to bring her water; she doesn't even want water. She just wants an extra few moments with Audrey. Well, I'm jealous because she's *my* daughter and she prefers someone else—even if only for those few minutes. It's strange. . . . You marry someone hoping everything will work out, but because you've invested many more years in the children, part of you is also thinking: *but not that well.*"

"I'm jealous, too," said Audrey, "because the children are not mine. There are many times when I wish they had been born to me. I suspect that wouldn't be my fantasy if I'd had children of my own, but I didn't—and so it is. Jessie and Jed call me Audrey, and I've accepted that, although—you asked me to be candid— I'd love it if they called me Mother. But they do have a mother, and she'd have a fit if she ever heard them call me that."

And the children? If any member of this new family has reason to be jealous, it is the child who sees some stranger enter the family and lay claim to the affections of its members. The easy acceptance Audrey Kendall met with is atypical. Most children are wary of new relationships. More often than not, they will want to disrupt them. Even when they like the incoming adult, the children must struggle with feelings of divided loyalty. (If I like my stepmother, am I being unfaithful to my mother—or, in some cases, to the memory of my mother?)

"It is more than a question of divided loyalty," stresses Dena Whitebook, associate director of counseling at the American Institute of Family Relations. "The children are feeling absolute confusion and guilt."

If the new marriage is entered into following a divorce between the natural parents, remarriage writes an end to the fantasy that Mommy and Daddy will get back together. Many youngsters will try, some subtly and others quite blatantly, to break up the marriage.

"All stepchildren are children of trauma," believes Joseph Chuman. "They have all lost a parent, either through death or divorce."

But what if the nonresident parent remains very involved in the life of the child, if there is a fair amount of visiting back and forth?

"Kids are self-centered," Chuman contends. "Even if the visiting parent shows deep concern, the child senses that this concern and love was not great enough for the parents to have kept the marriage intact."

Having been hurt once, many stepchildren are wary and jealous of the incoming adult in their lives, someone who will also receive much attention and affection from their parent.

WHAT DO YOU DO IF YOU FIND YOU ARE DEALING WITH JEALOUSY?

It must be confronted and acknowledged. For John Miles, acknowledgment has led him to be more tolerant of the time Audrey and his children spend together, to be supportive of their relationships with one another.

If it becomes clear that the children are directing their energies toward sabotaging the marriage, the parent must help the youngsters accept the fact that he or she is committed to the marriage bond (which need not mean a lessening of his or her commitment to the child) and that any attempts to play parent against stepparent will not succeed.

Presenting a United Front

Where one of the adults is an instant parent, both should be wary that the child does not honor his or her own parent while making an "unperson" of the stepparent. You will often find the natural parent taking an authoritarian role (after all, the parent reasons, it is *my* child) or acting as intermediary between child and stepparent. The natural parent may fear that the structure of the newly formed family is so precarious that, without such strong support, it will crumble. Nonetheless, the natural parent must step aside, believes Dr. Meltzer, and allow a relationship to develop between the stepparent and the child. To exclude the stepparent does a disservice to everyone in the family. Stepparents who are treated as intruders have little alternative but to protect themselves. In so doing, a stepparent becomes emotionally alienated from the rest of the family.

Such a contest for control is going on in the home of Luis Arenal; nobody is likely to emerge a winner.

Luis emigrated from his native Cuba to the United States with his first wife, Inez. Seven years of a bitter marriage culminated in an even more vitriolic divorce. Inez remained in Florida with Tony and Maria, the two children of the marriage.

Luis moved to Poughkeepsie and became manager of an apartment complex. Two years later, he married Marilyn. She was in her thirties, American born, a secretary. She had not been married before.

From the day she learned of Luis' remarriage, Inez refused him any contact with the children. Phone calls were intercepted, letters returned unopened. Aware of her husband's pain, Marilyn grumbled about "that bitch of a woman." Luis shrugged his shoulders, shifting the weight of the world. He carried his sadness stoically. It was a private burden. "Life changes," he pronounced. "I have been through a lot and I have learned how life is."

Life is unpredictable.

Five years had gone by in this fashion when, one day, Luis received a phone call from Tony. It was the first communication between father and son in half a decade. "I want to know who you are," said the thirteen-year-old boy. "I'll be arriving by plane on Sunday."

Thus, five years after her wedding day, Marilyn found herself facing the reality of living with her stepchild. (Such a change of situation is not uncommon. A youngster whose custody has been granted to one parent may decide one day to move in with the other parent. This change of heart typically takes place during adolescence. The other side of this situation occurs when the custodial parent—generally the mother—wakes up one day to find her little boy is now six feet two inches tall and a teen-ager, one she is having trouble controlling. At this point, she sends the boy to live with his father. The man or woman who marries a parent who has minimal contact with the children must recognize the possibility that distant relationships will grow closer. Children can and do relocate from the home of one parent to the residence of the other.)

As she awaited the arrival of Luis' son, Marilyn grew very nervous. After all, she knew nothing about the boy. What kind of person was Tony? How would it feel to have a teen-ager living in their home? What would it be like to have a son? Would Tony like her?

Her fears were well founded. Prepared to grapple with instant parenthood, Marilyn found herself written off as an instant stranger. In the two years he has lived in her home, Tony has never once asked Marilyn's opinion nor has he responded to her directives.

"Don't go out after dinner. It's too dark out," she will say.

"I don't have to listen to you; you're not my parent," he replies.

Luis offers Marilyn no support. It is he who makes all decisions concerning the youngster. Father and son often speak to one another in Spanish, again placing Marilyn at a distance from them. Having regained a son he thought lost to him, Luis seems jealous of anyone (including his wife) intruding on the relationship. In *this* home, he has made it clear, he is The Parent. Marilyn has found herself living with *two* hostile persons. She wonders, did she ever have a place here?

In retaliation, Marilyn now refuses to perform any of the chores traditionally associated with the mother role. She will not wait dinner for the boy. She insists he do his own laundry. "I may not be his mother," she states with defiance, "but I sure as hell refuse to become his maid." She is considering abandoning the role of wife as well.

The question of how discipline is handled in the stepfamily, the matter of who imposes rules and regulations, is dealt with at greater length in Chapter 10. In brief summary, family counselors agree it is essential for the stepparent to have the strong support of the natural parent if any sort of step relationship is to succeed. At the very least, husband and wife should decide on who metes out discipline (if it is to be a one-sided activity) and how rules are to be enforced.

The merged family, no matter that its rules differ from those in any previous or present home occupied by the children, must be *seen* as united if that appearance is ever to become a fact.

Petty Daily Annoyances Can Lead to Serious Resentment

THE LAUNDRY AND OTHER HOUSEHOLD CHORES

"I felt I was becoming a maid. . . ." The instant parent, in particular, seems overburdened by chores, and undervalued. "I couldn't *believe* all the laundry," recalled Audrey Kendall.

A woman who married a man many years her senior, and became "instant washerwoman" to stepsons who visited the couple during weekends and college vacations, also spoke to this point. "I wanted to like the boys, and I wanted at the same time to respect them. I expected the same from them. There were some unpleasant incidents early on and, for too long, I was willing to put up with behavior that really rankled—like waking up on Saturday and finding a load of laundry dumped outside the bedroom door. Quietly, I would take the laundry downstairs and do it; I didn't want to bring my problems to my husband. I was *not* going to be a nagging second wife. But the boys were smart. When they realized they had hit upon a source of annoyance to me, they compounded it. Finally came the day I decided that if I was going to be a slave, they'd have no respect for me. I took the boys by the hand into the laundry room and firmly demonstrated how to run the machines. My stepsons were eighteen and twenty at the time!"

THE STEREO AND OTHER NOISES

"I told the judge it was incompatibility," said a fifty-year-old man who had just written an end to his second marriage. "How could I say it was that damned stereo?"

Following the death of his first wife, this childless widower wed a woman with three children, two of them adolescents. He was unprepared for the noise, the constant activity, the scuffles among siblings, the slamming of the refrigerator door, the chaos that replaced the order of his life.

Unwilling to rail at each and every provocation lest he seem unreasonable, this gentleman centered his anger on an object—the stereophonic phonograph that was on, it seemed to him, at all hours and at highest volume, blaring electric rock into the very crevices of the house. Why didn't the kids tune that damn machine down—or, better still, off?

"That's the way children are," his wife told him, at the same time admonishing the youngsters to curb the noise. But she never recognized the problem as a serious one. Over the years, she'd become accustomed to noise. For a time, her older son had played percussion in the school orchestra. Her daughter had gone through a period of lessons on the electric guitar. Sometimes, it seemed, she didn't even hear the phonograph blasting away.

"A man can't even read the paper in this house," her husband

complained, and opted for the single life again. He now counsels
friends who contemplate remarriage: "Not everyone can make it
as a parent. Think before you step!"

A similar warning was sounded by a society matron who
married her husband, a widower, when his son was seven. The
young man is now twenty-three and, his stepmother stated with
obvious relief, no longer living with the family. When he was
home, she noted, there had always been household help to tend to
his needs. "[Nevertheless,] when I married my husband," she
said, "and I must tell you I am not particularly fond of children, I
intellectualized that I would accept his son. I want to stress that
no matter that you intellectually accept this, no matter how much
intelligence you bring to it, if you don't like children, having a
child around and underfoot (even for weekends) can get on your
nerves.

"I think stepparenting is very individual," she summed up her
feelings. "If you like children very much, you can draw close to
other people's children."

THE SCHOOLS AND OTHER COMMUNITY INVOLVEMENTS

First-time parents of school-age youngsters are thrust quickly
into a world of classes and other child-centered activities. Many
give little thought to the fact that they will be expected to function
within this world. They find themselves uncomfortable when
called upon to deal with teachers, principals, and the protocol of
educational institutions. While this seldom remains an overriding
problem, it is one that the instant parent must confront early on.

"Arthur and I had been married three weeks when we received
a note from my stepdaughter Lisa's teacher," recalled Helen, a
handsome woman who recently returned to school, after ten years
as a full-time housewife, to pursue a master's degree in library sci-
ence. "The teacher asked that we come in to see her. The appointment was for a weekday afternoon, when Arthur would be at
work, so it was up to me to go. It all made good sense, but I
remember, as though ten years ago were yesterday, how nervous I
felt about entering that fifth-grade classroom. Where was the
room, I wanted to know. On what floor? Turn right at what corri-
dor? And who was I, after all, to presume to act as Lisa's parent?

"I found the room and Lisa's teacher without great difficulty. I introduced myself. Lisa was my stepdaughter, I blurted—too quickly and too loudly.

"Lisa had been acting up a bit, her teacher informed me. She hadn't been doing her homework assignments with care, and she'd been surly. Was this how the child usually behaved, I wondered? Did I have a problem child on my hands?

"Lisa was asked to join us. I didn't know what role to play. I wanted my stepdaughter to see me as a friend, someone on her side, and I wanted the teacher to see me as a responsible adult—a parent. I probably came across as indecisive and satisfied neither Lisa nor her teacher. And I was annoyed at Arthur who had placed me in this position. I felt he should have been there. Yet I know I would have been upset if *he* had kept the appointment, as Lisa's Real Parent, and if I had remained at home.

"It took me a long time to be able to deal comfortably with teachers, the PTA, Girl Scouts, and car pools, and talking to other children's parents on the phone. I now think I would have found it helpful had Arthur and I attended some of these activities together until I got the hang of it, but I don't know if there would have been an easy way for me, as a single woman, to metamorphose into an active, involved parent to, as it turned out, a very nice young woman. (Lisa's problems in school were temporary, a reaction to the many changes in *her* life.) I was shell-shocked for a time—in all probability we all were—but we came through."

ADJUSTING TO GHOSTS IN THE HOME

Whether the new family is formed following the death of one parent of the original unit or after the dissolution of the first marriage by divorce, those who enter the step unit must develop a means of living with the ghost (the parent who does not play a daily, on-stage role in the life of the child but who nonetheless is ever-present). When that ghost is alive and well, adjustment to its effects on the family can be very difficult.

It continues to be so for Audrey Kendall and John Miles. "Every once in a while, I fall into the trap of thinking about myself as the children's real mother," said their stepmother. "They have come to mean so much to me . . . and then I'm brought up sharply by something their real mother does, and I have to face the conflict in our life styles and our values."

For the sake of the children, Audrey had developed a cordial relationship with Renee, who is their mother and a woman Audrey disapproves of and would prefer to ignore. "I'm an optimist and I entered this marriage believing it would work out smoothly," she confessed, "but I continue to find I underestimated the complexities, the conflicting loyalties the children have. When there's tension between Renee and me, Jed and Jessie feel it and they react by doing something to hurt me . . . because they need to reassure themselves that they're not being unfaithful to their own mother. I try not to tell them how I feel about her, but I'm only human and sometimes she makes it rather difficult."

Jessie and Jed see their mother every other weekend. She picks them up at their home. One Friday afternoon when Renee arrived, she was carrying a large cage that contained one baby boa constrictor coiled around a rock.

"It's for Jed," Renee announced. "He's always wanted a snake."

"I can't *stand* snakes," Audrey recounted, recoiling even as she spoke of the incident. "I wouldn't have been able to sleep at night, just knowing there was one in our apartment. Jed was understandably excited by his present. I didn't want to take his joy away, yet I knew this was something I could not tolerate. And I told Jed no, the snake could not stay.

"Later that evening, I cried more bitterly than at any other time in my life, because Renee had forced me to be an evil stepmother and I had been trying *so hard* to be nice. Damn it, why hadn't she bought Jed a snake during the years he lived with *her!*"

The absent parent lives with the stepfamily every day, and the man or woman who considers entering a stepfamily must recognize this. Thelma Kaplan, marriage, family, and child counselor in San Gabriel, California, has found that the first issue to be dealt with in stepfamilies is helping people let go of the ghosts of marriages past, be they dead or alive, helping them come to terms with old relationships so they can accept and enjoy the new.

To the instant parent, the ghostly visits seem particularly unfair. She has included no similar specters in the baggage she's brought with *her.*

IF YOU MARRY THE NONCARETAKING PARENT, DOES THE TAG "INSTANT PARENT" APPLY TO YOU?

The children live with their custodial parent and visit your home during alternate weekends . . . or Christmas and Easter vacations . . . or sometime in the summer months. You don't have to deal with them daily. How do they regard you: are you mother's husband . . . father's wife . . . are you any sort of parent at all?

It is unlikely that you'll be viewed as a parent figure for some time, but your importance to the children *can* grow as they get to know you and as you involve yourself in their lives. It is you who must decide the extent of your involvement. The possibilities range from total acceptance of a meaningful relationship with the children to no acknowledgment of a need to be involved.

Although there is no one tried and true, pat answer, it is important that husband and wife discuss their expectations before they waltz into matrimony. They may be surprised to discover that each has a very different perception of the roles that each will play.

The clash of conflicting expectations can cause a good deal of pain, as Kevin and Sarah Geary found out. Two years following the breakup of a five-year marriage, Kevin Geary married Sarah, a young, attractive student nurse whom he met at work. He is a hospital administrator. His daughter Meghan lives with her mother and visits with her father from Friday through Sunday every other weekend.

Kevin's expectation: "I felt terrible about the divorce. Part of my motivation to remarry was to establish a new home in which I could be the good parent again. When I met Sarah, I pictured her as loving Meghan, as any mother would love a child. I thought I conveyed how much Meghan meant to me. If Sarah accepted me, I believed, in the same way she had to accept my child."

Sarah's expectation: "When Kevin and I were courting, I never hesitated about going into the marriage because he had a daughter. I was much more concerned about the difference in our religions and the fact that Kevin was a divorced man. *And I knew Meghan would not be living with us, so I downplayed her importance and impact on our lives.* In the beginning, I just wanted to be a wonderful wife, and good to Kevin's child."

In real life, however: "I found myself becoming very resentful of Meghan," said Sarah. "I was jealous of the time Kevin spent with her when I thought he should have been at home with me. I resented the hours he put in on the thruway Friday evenings, driving to pick Meghan up and bring her to our place, while I waited dinner and the food grew cold."

Kevin interjects: "Sarah acted as if I was having a ball on that thruway. It never occurred to her that I was tired after a long day's work followed by an interminable drive, that I didn't relish being involved in weekend traffic but I had no choice. It was either drive to pick up Meghan or give up the chance to spend time with my daughter. Finally, I'd arrive home exhausted, hoping to find a haven, and I'd find myself confronted by a harridan."

Sarah: "I didn't like Meghan's manners. I didn't like the way she behaved at table. I think I was deeply involved in having the little girl be a good reflection of *me,* so I took on the role of disciplinarian. Her doting father wasn't going to come on strong, not when he had to use the weekend to make up to Meghan for all the guilt that he carried about not being with her during the week. At some point, I realized I didn't want the disciplinarian role. I really think the wicked stepmother is not a myth. I felt put upon, cast as that character, and it was then that I decided Meghan was *not* my child. She's Kevin's responsibility, not mine. Let *him* discipline her."

Kevin's reality: "After six years, I have come to accept the fact that my expectations could not possibly be met. It is a continuing source of pain."

"I worried terribly about taking on three children. Yet I have found few problems once I accepted the fact that a weekend stepmother is not a mother no matter how much she yearns to assume a maternal role," wrote Jean Baer in *The Second Wife.*

There *is* another role to play. One stepmother suggests it is that of mature counselor and concerned friend. "I am far less emotionally involved with my stepdaughter Anita than is her father," said this woman. "He often makes decisions about what she can and cannot do based on his emotional reactions. I am able to stand back and take a much more detached view of matters that involve her, and sometimes I think I draw father and daughter together.

"When her father makes a decision that Anita deems unreasonable, like not allowing her to join her friends on an overnight ski trip, Anita is likely to stomp off to her room and slam the door. Her father retreats to the den. A pall settles over the household. So I knock on the door to Anita's room, enter, and explain to her that her father may have behaved in a seemingly arbitrary manner because he did not know how else to express his fears for her safety, and his concern.

"Later, I find a time to remind my husband that his daughter is a capable skier, and to offer my opinion that she ought to be given permission to go along with the group on a supervised activity. It's not that I am the personification of reason itself, but I *am* able to have a different perspective on what's going on in the family, precisely because Anita is *not* my daughter. I'm delighted when I find my intercession has been helpful.

"Anita has brought life into my world," said this woman. "On the weekends she is with us, she just steps into the foyer and, in less than a minute it seems, our home is filled with all the young boys and girls in the neighborhood.

"Whatever would Christmas be without her!"

2

Your Place or Mine?

Deciding Where to Set Up the Blended Household

For the remarried couple, the decision concerning where to set up home—your place or mine?—rests on a good deal more than which house has southern exposure and which apartment offers cross-ventilation. Where others look for termites, reweds search out ghosts. Does the Spirit of Marriage Past stalk the hallways? If so, there is danger to the present marriage.

On the face of it, having the less encumbered partner join the more established household seems a very reasonable idea, as when a childless spouse (the instant parent) or the parent who no longer has custody of the children moves into the home already occupied by the larger unit of the merging family. It seems an intelligent plan: the house is large enough; it is furnished; it fits the family. The children are nestled all snug in their beds. *Only the intruder tosses and turns.*

Intruder. Time and again that word crops up in conversation with men and women who live in blended households formed by having one marriage partner (with or without other members of that family) move into the home of the other spouse.

The theme is echoed by P. T. Lowe in her book, *The Cruel Stepmother*. The author shares her reaction on moving into the home of her new husband: "I was uncertain as to my attitude, frankly. First of all, it was very big, and I was intimidated. In it had lived the previous housekeeper—my husband's first wife. In it had lived Andrew [her stepson]. It was I, really, who was the intruder. And as I look back on it now (at the time I never analyzed my unease) I never really got over the sense of being an interloper."

Manfred, a bachelor until he reached his mid-thirties, was uneasy about the living arrangement he'd agreed to when he and Janet, a divorced mother of two, decided to marry. Manfred was to move, bag and baggage, into Janet's home. But *first,* like Linus, he brought in his blanket.

"Even before I moved out of my apartment," said Manfred, "Janet and I made a lot of changes in her house, to make it somewhat *my* place. We redid the master bedroom, added some of my furniture to the den and to some of the other rooms. The first thing that went on the bed was my blanket, not to make the room more attractive but to stake a claim: *this is mine; I belong here.* I *had* to make that statement.

"It didn't work," he continued. "Every time the children came into the room, I felt they were accusing me—'what are you doing here, acting as if you belong, in our house, in our mother's bedroom?' I felt their accusations: I was the intruder. When a place just down the street came on the market, Janet sold her house and we bought the new house together. The children's routines of school and neighborhood activities go on as always, but my life has changed greatly—for the better."

"I felt like a stranger in someone else's house," was the way another instant father described a situation that was similar to the one in which Manfred found himself. He, too, found the situation was improved only when the family changed its residence.

In Chevy Chase, Maryland, John continues to make his home in the white-shingled colonial that belongs to his wife Karla, the house in which she and her three children (and *their* father, before the divorce) lived for fifteen years. "But I don't like it," John says. He gave up a studio apartment in Washington, D.C. (where he works) along with his bachelorhood. "I cannot get over the feeling of being a boarder in Karla's home," he admits. "On my income, I could never afford to live in a house like this and I know it. The children are aware of it, too, and I have no doubt all the neighbors know it. Yet I can't think of any sensible options. I doubt I could have handled the rent for a large-size apartment in the District, which we would have needed if Karla and her youngsters came to live with me. And then there's the question of education. The schools are better in Chevy Chase. Still, even though the arrangement we came up with—my moving into Karla's house —makes sense, I wish there had been a reasonable alternative. . . ."

A marriage counselor whom we asked to consider John's situation offers a suggestion: Might John and Karla have moved to a community in which nobody knew their history, knew who paid the rent, and in fact might they not have arranged to share the expenses of a new residence (It need not be a fifty-fifty deal, she stresses), making the house John and Karla's place, instead of simply Karla's?

More than the discomfort of the moving-in parent is at issue here. It is difficult for someone who feels like an intruder to also see himself or herself as some sort of authority figure, as an integral member of the household. "If it is at all possible (and I recognize that often it is not) and you can afford it, it's better to get a new place for the new relationship," counsels psychiatrist Clifford J. Sager, director of the Remarriage Consultation Service of the Jewish Board of Family and Children's Services.

Dr. Sager tells of a man who came to see him: "The man owned a good house, his mortgage was all paid up, he was comfortable. So, as part of the divorce agreement, he kept the house and furniture. When he remarried, his new wife moved in. She rearranged some of the furniture. The man's children arrived for a weekend visit. They took one look around the living room and commented loudly, 'Gee, why'd you change it? Everything looked a lot better the way Mom had the place fixed up.' "

Remarrieds who move into an established household find such comparisons inevitable—and rankling. Said one stepmother whose predecessor walked out on her husband and children, "Every time some change I make in the house is criticized—and believe me I can't move an ash tray without it being cause for discussion—I want to answer the kids' editorials by saying, 'Sure, your mom had everything arranged so well, she even arranged her departure neatly.' But I bite my tongue and go on about my business."

EVICTING GHOSTS

When the former parent has died, the ghost is harder to evict from the premises than when remarriage has followed divorce.

Susan married Ben Neuman, a widower with two children, and found she'd moved into a house that was a shrine to his late wife, Esther. Susan sat on Esther's couch, dusted Esther's piano (Susan did not play), cooked in Esther's kitchen, did the laundry for Esther's children, and sometimes wondered if she was keeping Esther's husband sexually satisfied.

"I liked it better the way it was," Ben remarked every time Susan made some change in her living environment, something that reflected her taste, her judgment. The children picked up the refrain. Susan moved a lamp from one side of the room to another; her stepson complained he could no longer read in his favorite chair because there wasn't enough light.

"Light," remarks Susan, "was not the issue."

Susan's taste runs to leather and chrome; Esther was reflected in velvet—but velvet of quality, which made the furnishings all the more difficult to replace. "I never wanted to blot out the memory of Ben's wife and the children's mother," said Susan, "and I like to think Esther would not have wished to destroy *me*. Nevertheless, that's what was happening. Esther's house perpetuated her presence. It was a large enough home, but it was too crowded for me."

When Susan suggested selling the house, Ben accused her of being unreasonable. After years of struggling to meet mortgage payments, Ben finally had reached the comfortable situation of being able to afford the house. More than that, it had become a bargain. At the same time real estate costs had skyrocketed. Any move would be very expensive. . . .

Calmly and deliberately Susan asked Ben, "How much is this marriage worth?"

Ben agreed to look for another residence. The house the Neumans moved into *was* expensive, as Ben had predicted, but rising real estate values had brought a good price for his old house, too. The difference between the two was not significant. The new home is an eclectic blend of old and new. An Eames chair sits on an Aubusson rug, next to the velvet sofa. An antique brass lamp rests on a sparkling glass table. Susan's stepson finds there is enough light to read by. The old and new do not clash. Rather, the present is enhanced by the past. What is true for the house has become true for the family.

To members of the blending family who find themselves considering the question of "Your place or mine?" family experts suggest that there is a third and ofttimes better choice: "Ours."

Family counselor Dena K. Whitebook stands out in playing down the importance of where the family makes its home. "How any stepparenting situation works out depends on the couple's self-esteem," the counselor believes. "The higher the self-esteem of the adults, the better the adjustment. The need of a stepparent to make quick, drastic changes in the environment is a sign of low self-esteem.

"In a new home," Whitebook continued, "everybody is still in turmoil. They are not starting out from scratch. The new home does not make the children feel less displaced. True, the rivalry with a former parent is a little more diminished. A new home may help somewhat, but it is *not* a panacea.

"I say 'may' advisedly," she added. "It may not make any difference at all. Where the remarried family lives is not the core problem. I feel that the core problem is in the child's relationship with the natural parent and fears about his own identity: his fear of the unknown and of what this new family will be like." The child, Whitebook feels, needs reassurance more than he needs change. . . .

This is precisely what led Jeanne and Jerry Kahan to decide on staying on in the same village, the same house in which Jeanne had lived during the twelve years she'd been married to Paul, with whom she had had three children. "We felt it was more important to provide continuity for my children," explained Jeanne. A social worker, Jeanne is very aware of feelings. "We were particularly concerned about my son Josh, who was ten, and what moving away from his friends and school would mean to him. My two younger children, we felt, had fewer ties and could be more flexible."

Jerry's children, from his previous marriage, lived an hour's ride away. They could, and did, visit often.

Paul, Jeanne's ex-husband, had married a woman who'd been a friend of Jeanne's before the divorce. They'd all belonged to the same clubs and organizations and they continued to see each other at meetings and social functions. (Paul had moved into the house of *his* new wife, less than a mile from his former home.) This came close to being a textbook illustration of "civilized divorce and remarriage in the latter part of the twentieth century."

Only Jerry was a newcomer to this community. "I felt I had tagged on to Jeanne and Paul's lives, not that Jeanne and I were building one together," said Jerry. "We often showed up at the same parties that Paul and his wife were at or ran into one another on line for the movies or at the supermarket. It was all too amicable. Paul got into the habit of 'dropping by' the house frequently and without notice. He 'just wanted to see his children,' he would say, or he 'just thought it would be a good idea to pick up the kids and drive them over to Burger King.' . . . He seemed so at ease, so right, sitting there in his former kitchen, chatting easily with his former wife, surrounded by his children, my stepchildren. . . .

"How can I put it tactfully?" asked Jerry. "Let's just say a move was deemed prudent."

The Kahans sold the house that Paul built and relocated the family in a completely different community. Said Jeanne, "We moved into a new house in which no rooms have previous names. No kids are replacing other kids. We even have rooms that belong to Jerry's children; they know they're welcome here. In contrast, when my children visit their father's home, all the rooms in that house have names. They belong to their stepmother's children, and those kids are displaced during visiting weekends to make room for mine. This way—the way that Jerry and I have arrived at—is better."

WHEN EVERYBODY NEEDS A ROOM: REAL ESTATE CONSIDERATIONS
FOR THE HIS-AND-HER FAMILY

In an excellent article, "Myths That Intrude on the Adaptation of the Stepfamily," sociologist Gerda L. Schulman observed: "Although the combination family consists of two existing family units, one subgroup is usually considered the basic family and is accorded the dominant position. The difference in status does not appear to depend on whether the subgroup is headed by the mother or the father, but rather on whose house becomes the new family's home and which of the parents is the dominant partner."

In the blended family, struggles for dominance can and do take place over just about everything having to do with possession, as the following story illustrates.

It made sense for Catherine, a widow, to move with her two children from a city apartment to the home of her new husband, George, and his three children, whose mother had died two years earlier. The house was large and comfortable; it sat on six acres and was located in a rural community in which George, a lawyer, had established a successful practice.

Before they could be married and combine families, however, Catherine and George decided they'd have to make some changes in his house. "If there was one thing of which I was certain, it was that I'd never sleep in the same room that had been occupied by George and his late wife," said Catherine. "I sensed that not only I but my stepchildren—in particular Eileen, George's teen-age daughter—would be uncomfortable with that arrangement. We called in an architect who designed a new bedroom built out over the garage for George and me, and redid the old master bedroom for Eileen. George's two boys share a bedroom, an earlier arrangement they asked to have continued, and my daughter took over Eileen's former room. We converted a guest room into a bedroom for my son. The den now serves as a guest room. So there is plenty of space."

And yet . . .

The standard of living for Catherine and her children had decidedly improved, yet the youngsters constantly complained that life had been better in the city. The grass about the house was green, but this was not their turf.

They struggled to make it so. As often is the case when two families combine, each brings some belongings from the past into the present household. Catherine left most of her furniture behind, but brought with her the family's chinaware, silver table service, crystal stemware, and many daily household articles. The cupboard in George's home was equally well outfitted.

It didn't take long for a power play to develop between the two groups of children, with advantage points gained by the team whose family dishes appeared on the table for dinner, whose knife and fork flanked each plate.

"That may *sound* petty," declared Catherine, "but I assure you it was serious. For my children, the dishes represented their position in our combination family. When a glass or a dish from their former home was used, it signified: 'We have contributed something to this place. We belong here.' My stepchildren's insistence on continuing to use whatever was familiar to them was a negation of my children's claim. My stepchildren were replying: 'No, you do not.' "

George, who had been listening, now smiled wryly and added, almost as an aside, "Five years of family therapy stand behind that brilliant instant analysis.

"But we *have* come a long way as a family," he continued in all seriousness. "No, we haven't held a mammoth garage sale and gotten rid of all our belongings, Catherine's and mine. We talked about holding one, though, and decided we *wanted* a link with our pasts. Much had been good. But we wouldn't let our separate histories keep us from becoming a united family. We weren't just talking about place settings, you know, and we were clear about that, too. We *were* talking about merging our families into a workable unit—something *we* needed to work on. First, we had to recognize that no one was an intruder, no one a gracious host. Each unit has something of value to bring to the combined family.

"To continue the dinner-table analogy," said George, "we find we are able to blend our table settings, which we now do. We also add to our home, when need or desire dictates it, some new items that reflect our mutual taste. And sometimes we even forget what came into the home by which door. Those are the moments that make all the struggle and self-conscious attempts at unification worth while."

3

Coming to Terms with Terminology

The Who's Who of the reconstructed family often reads more like a suspense novel than a reference work. Who is the lady of the house? Is she Mom? Stepmom? Helen? Aunt Helen? or, as is often the case, is she simply referred to as "she"? What is her role? Is it acknowledged by her title? (The same questions can be asked about the male head of the household.)

One stepmother reports that her husband's children have come around to calling her their *stepped-on* mother because, they admit with humor, over the years she has taken so much abuse. They also call her by her given name, Betty. She would have preferred "Mother," but recognizes with some sadness she is *not* the children's mother. For the time being, and for want of a more precise title that indicates the closeness of their relationship, "Betty" will have to do.

What's in a name? Those who work with and study sequential families concede that a lot more than the title itself is involved in the question of names. Position, acceptance, respect, and love may be reflected in the appellation the stepchild bestows upon his or her stepparent. While recognizing the significance of familial titles, they nevertheless caution those who live in step not to force the issue.

"It is the basic relationship between the stepparent and stepchild that is important, not the names they use to address one another," writes Richard A. Gardner in *The Parents' Book About Divorce.* "Parents should not try to force a child to use a name that he or she is not comfortable with. Often this is done to provide an appearance of intimacy and closeness for a relationship that may be somewhat deficient."

Jeanette Lofas, coauthor of *Living in Step,* tells of a woman who insisted her stepdaughter call her Mom. "I do all the things a mother does," this woman felt. "I feed her, shop with her and for her, do her laundry. . . ."

"But the girl, who spent the major part of her time in the home of her father and stepmother, still saw 'Mother' as the title for her biological mother," Lofas continued, "and so tensions arose over the name.

"Do not insist on the title that is *your due,*" counsels Jeanette Lofas, who is herself a stepmother and learned the hard way many of the rules she now hands down to others. "You are not your stepchild's mother or father—no matter how close the relationship. On the other hand, if the stepchild naturally takes to calling you Mother or Dad, the youngster need not be corrected."

Often, children who would like to call their surrogate parents Mom or Dad are stopped from doing so by the knowledge (intuited or declared) that the real parent would view this as the supreme disloyalty. "I just kept waiting for my daughter to call my former husband's current wife Mother," said one angry woman. "That would have been the ultimate violation. That woman took my husband; over my dead body will I let her steal my child."

If you sense your stepchild is under similar pressure, you can lift some of the burden by letting her or him know your relationship rests on a good deal more than a choice of titles.

WHAT'S IN A NICKNAME?

There *is* a middle ground, report many families, and that is to encourage the stepchildren to come up with a nickname for the adult who is not the parent.

"I'm very much in favor of nicknames," declared a young woman who for the first three years following her marriage to a divorced father found herself diminished to a pronoun by his two sons, sixteen and nineteen at the time of the marriage. "*She* wouldn't let me take the car out," the older son would report as soon as his father returned home from the office. "I told *her* it would be okay with you, Dad."

Today, symbolizing a much improved relationship, the woman has become "Chubs" to her stepsons. Model-slim, she is constantly kidded about her devotion to her calorie counter; hence, the nickname. "The nickname shows intimacy, is different from what others call me, and yet isn't Mom," she says. "I like it."

For traditionalists who find themselves uncomfortable with being addressed on a first-name basis by members of the younger generation, an appropriate nickname can be the answer.

Professor Kevin Connor declares, "I am not the father of my stepchildren, and I would feel uncomfortable having them call me by a title that infers we have that relationship. In addition, my own children often join the household and I would not want them to hear someone else's children address me as Father." Solution: the professor's stepchildren have taken to calling him D.C. (for Doctor Connor).

It is not unusual for children to select nicknames that are similar to, but differ from, the names they call their own parents. "For many years," said Phil, a television actor, "my stepdaughter called me Pops; her own father is Daddy. That was fine. Then her mother and I had a mutual child. He's taken to calling me Poppa, which is his two-year-old's adaptation of Pops, and I get a great kick out of it. I'd be a lot less happy, I'll admit, if my stepdaughter had referred to me as Phil and my son picked *that* up."

Which is why ex-marine Tommy Rivers asked his stepson John to start calling him Dad.

"Even though I'm raising the boy and I love him, I wasn't trying to make him forget he has another father," said Rivers. "He hears from his father at least once a year, during the man's annual drying out, and I don't put John's father down to him or make a point that I'm the one who's raising him. But when John's mother and I found we were going to have a baby of our own, it became important to me that John begin speaking to me as Dad. I didn't want the baby to pick up what he hears from John and, when he began to speak, to start calling me Tommy."

"THIS IS JEDDY'S . . . ER"

When the rearrangement of the family is still new and strange to its members, they find it difficult as well to define themselves to the outside world.

For a year before they decided to marry, Stan Grant lived with Meryl and her son, Jeddy, twelve, and daughter, Leora, nine. The scene that follows was played often in their home.

The phone rings. Stan moves across the room and lifts the telephone receiver. A young boy's voice is heard.

Young boy: "Is Jeddy at home?"

Stan: "No, he's out."

Young boy: "Oh, is this his father?"

          [Possible variation: "Who is this?"]

Stan: "No. This is Jeddy's . . . er . . ."

Mother's friend? Mother's lover? Make it simple: This is Mr. Grant.

"I never knew *what* was the right answer," said Grant. "Then Meryl and I were married. Now I'm able to respond, 'This is Jeddy's stepfather.' Jeddy, on the other hand, continues to introduce me as his 'er.' One Saturday, we were having lunch at a nearby restaurant—Jeddy, Leora, my daughter Barbara, Meryl, and I—when one of Jeddy's classmates stopped by our table. 'This is . . . ,' Jeddy started to explain, and looked about the table. Then, with an encompassing gesture he declared, 'This is the family.' "

THE SURNAME DILEMMA

"We've come up against some mildly awkward moments concerning the fact that, as members of a stepfamily, we carry different surnames," Grant continued. "Jeddy's family name is Harris. When people who know Jeddy have to speak with me, on the phone or in person, ten to one they'll greet me as Mr. Harris. I then have to correct them. Generally, I find the person I'm speaking to is more embarrassed than I."

Not only is the stepparent bothered by this problem of names, so are the natural mothers, for with remarriage they often change their surnames and are not immediately recognizable as their children's mothers.

"When my son, Bill Stone, graduated as salutatorian of his class at college," said one mother, "my son's father and his wife, Trudy, were there as Mr. and Mrs. Stone. I was there as Anne Hudson. Everybody kept congratulating *them* as Bill's parents, and I felt *I* was the other woman."

The surname dilemma, in another form, was confronted by a thirteen-year-old girl whose father had remarried following divorce, but whose mother had not. "I accepted the fact that my father was going to remarry," said the young girl. "I even liked the woman he'd chosen, but when she became Mrs. Walters I cringed. I mean, my own *mother* is Mrs. Walters. I think there ought to be a different name for second wives," she suggested. "At least, something like Mrs. Walters II."

Eventually, the members of the combination family work out what their roles will be and, along the way, assign titles that become familiar, if not altogether comfortable. The question of who calls whom what assumes much less importance than it did when the relationships were new and the family participants insecure.

What's in a name? "Last summer," shared a woman whose stepson visits the family on holidays and nine weeks during the summer, "my husband's son came to me and asked if he could call me Mom. 'Because you act like a mom,' he said. I was elated. 'Of course, you may call me whatever you like,' I told him, and gave him a hug. Now he alternates between Alice and Mom, but it doesn't matter which of the two he calls me. I know the thought is there."

4

The Blended, Merged, Combination, His-and-Hers Stepfamily

For want of an appropriate noun, an assortment of adjectives is used to describe the family in which each of the marriage partners is both a natural parent and a stepparent to children in the home. Conversely, in this household each child lives with one biological and one acquired parent and with other youngsters to whom the child is not related genetically but with whom he or she is expected to form a kinship relationship. To say that there will be problems of adjustment seems redundant. The difficulties practically shout for themselves.

Is it any wonder? We begin with two existing family units, each of which may include children of different sexes and ages, with different histories, loyalties, and needs. They are thrust together —generally with little or no preparation for the merger—and are nevertheless expected to get along and become one big happy family.

What they quickly become is one very crowded family. Typically, there are more kids per square foot; space is at a premium, and the children maneuver for both real and emotional turf. The oldest child in one family is moved to middle position or becomes the youngest in the combined family, losing status and authority. The favored youngest child finds herself or himself displaced by younger stepsiblings who seem to command a lot of attention from both parents in the home as well as from visitors. Suddenly, this child is expected to "act your age," to shoulder more responsibility as "big sister" or "big brother" or, as one stepchild complained, "an unpaid baby-sitter."

Children who have worked out their roles in their first families now must grapple again with questions of "Who am I?" and "Where do I fit in here?" Depending on such variables as the age and sex of the youngsters involved, the presence or absence of other, nonresident parents and, above all, depending on the strength of the partners' commitment to making this marriage work, the two families will find ways to live together in combination or they will dwell in the same home as warring factions.

Learning to Live as a Family: William and Marilyn

In a modest, three-story row house situated in a middle-class community outside of Boston, William and Marilyn Krogh and their six children (three of his, three of hers) are learning to live together. The couple has been married two years. Not unexpectedly, theirs is a busy household.

The rooms of the Krogh house are not large, but they are many, furnished with an amalgam of belongings from two households that have been tastefully combined. Orange and gold predominate among the colors in the sunny family room where Marilyn, William, and I sit on an afternoon in autumn, talking about their combined family. How did they come together and how are they meeting the challenge of step?

William, a broad, handsome man in his early forties, begins with the explanation, "I had to become a parent before I could become a stepparent."

Five years earlier, after fifteen years of marriage, William found himself catapulted into the role of sole functioning parent to three lively daughters: Laura, then fourteen, Tania, thirteen, and Michelle, seven. "I came home at my usual hour, six-thirty, on what I thought was going to be a normal weekday evening," he relates without emotion, "and found a note from my wife, Andrea, propped up on the piano. She was leaving, she'd written, going off with the man who was the children's pediatrician. She wished me luck. That was it. She also left notes for each of the girls. We've never had a word from her since. Nor has the doctor's family heard from him. He has two children, a boy and girl. His wife has tried to find him, with no success. It isn't all that difficult for people to disappear, if they really want to.

"This may sound naïve," William continued, "but I hadn't the foggiest notion that anything had been going on. This is the kind of thing you read about in the papers—you know the rest: it never happens to you. I was in a state of shock, but I also realized that I had to do something about the kids.

"But what? Up to that time, the girls' mother had been the parent who'd seen to all the child care routines—schools, clothing, food, church, even the girls' social lives. I didn't know where to begin. I'm an organizing type of person—that's just the way my mind works, in an orderly fashion—and so the first thing I did was to sit the children down and work out our schedules. 'We've got to eat, get through the day, and sleep,' I said. We drew up a list of how we were going to meet those requirements. For at least the first six months, however, I didn't meet their emotional needs. I was too emotionally unstable myself. I felt (I still do) insecure in handling and sharing their feelings."

The Child in the Place of the Parent

William acknowledges another mistake. "I allowed Laura, my oldest daughter, to take over the mother and wife role. Laura told the kids when to sit down and do their homework and saw to it that they practiced the piano. She'd give me lists of what to buy at the supermarket and she let me know when the lawn needed mowing. She modeled herself after her mother, and the rest of us went along, glad that someone had taken over.

"When I began to meet women and go out on dates, I felt I had to account to Laura about where I was going and when I'd be home. Marilyn and I met at a get-together of Parents Without Partners. When we decided to marry, it was something like going through a second divorce for me because my daughter had become a kind of wife."

The elevation of a child to the status of partner is not unusual in families headed by a single parent. It happens more frequently following the death of a parent than it does following a divorce where the no-longer-resident parent is likely to continue to play an influential role in the lives of the children and, hence, of the family. For the Krogh youngsters, abandonment by their mother has been similar to a death, only harsher. They wonder what they did (or didn't do) that caused her to leave them. They wonder if they'll ever see her again.

Typically, the child who takes over is the oldest one who is of the same sex as the absent parent. Women look to the oldest son to shoulder more burdens ("You're the man of the house now, you know"), and men are delighted, as was William Krogh, when homemaker responsibilities are taken on by a daughter. When the parent remarries, such older children have a hard time dropping the parenting half of their double lives (child/parent) and accepting a new authority figure. It is hard for them to revert to being children again.

Therapist Libby Walker, who was associated with the Remarriage Consultation Service of the Jewish Board of Family and Children's Service, New York, notes, "One of the findings in our clinic population is that, almost without exception, the oldest child who has been forced to take on responsibility has grown up a lot faster, even physically, than other children his or her age. Almost without exception, the oldest child of eleven or twelve appears fully three to four years older. It's sad; these youngsters have not been allowed to be children. Our job in therapy is to help them to be children again. It *can* be done, and when we succeed it's very rewarding."

"I was very concerned about Laura," said Marilyn. "When William and I talked about getting married, I worried more about how—and if—Laura would accept me (I was afraid she'd try to sabotage the marriage) than I did about how my children would take to William or adapt to living in a house with *six children*. I didn't even think all that much about six children (I think about it a lot now, I'll tell you; it's an awful lot of responsibility), but I had many fears about me and Laura."

Marilyn's only daughter, Julie, a carbon copy of her fair, hazel-eyed mother, had not yet blown out the candle on her first birthday cake when her parents were divorced. There were two older boys: Marc, almost six, and Gregory, nine. Marilyn was awarded custody of the children. Their father, an alcoholic, sent money into the household from time to less frequent time. His visits with the children were equally sporadic. He has not seen them once in the past year. During the four years that followed the divorce, Marilyn worked at a series of jobs—as a saleswoman, secretary, hostess at a restaurant—to support the children. She also studied to become a licensed real estate broker, and now works in a real estate office, part time.

"William and I began to make marriage plans," said Marilyn. "I strongly felt I could not move into his house. It took me a while to get him to understand my feelings (it was a roomy, comfortable house and the mortgage was paid), but it was clear to me that Laura had become mistress of that house. I wasn't sure I could or even *should* replace her.

"An alternative might have been for William and the children to move into my house, but there were many reasons that didn't seem wise. The obvious one was that my place was too small. There were going to be so many of us, we had to have a house where we weren't on top of one another. We weren't rich, but we each owned a home. With the proceeds from the sales of both houses, we bought this house because it has a lot of bedrooms, is in a good school district, and is in a city that is new to all of us."

The Kroghs arranged for Laura to stay on in her old neighborhood to complete her school year. She moved in with William's sister. This separation underscored the break between William and his daughter as heads of the household and gave each some time to get used to the new state of family affairs. The following fall, Laura joined the combined family. "Living with Laura has been *great*," said Marilyn. "None of the problems we anticipated ever happened. But I think the time apart was good for us."

Relating to Other People's Children

"On the other hand," William admitted, "*I* anticipated no problems in getting along with Marilyn's kids. I always thought of myself as a fairly easygoing person—I was even more hurt than angry after Andrea walked out on the family—but I have experienced more anger since coming up against Gregory, Marilyn's older boy, than I thought myself capable of.

"Gregory throws temper tantrums with regularity, which Marilyn dismisses as part and parcel of being an adolescent but which, for some reason, I feel called upon to respond to. Each of the two of us has placed our egos on the line to see who will come out the victor in each and every argument. I realize I might be having similar fights with my own teen-age son, but I don't think I'd be worrying about whether I really *liked* the boy or that he'd be constantly testing my commitment to him. Gregory and I are always wary of one another. We have an uneasy truce."

Clashes between the oldest stepchild and the stepparent of the same sex occur more frequently than in opposite-sex relationships. Psychologist Nina Cohen suggests that is because the oldest child of the same sex as the stepparent has the most loyalty to the biological parent who has been replaced.

William's favorite child in the family, after Laura, is Marc, Marilyn's middle child. They share interests. Marc looks up to William and likes to work with him on projects in the carpentry room that has been set up in the basement. William is enjoying having a son.

Often, the youngest child in stepfamilies is the favored child and becomes more quickly absorbed by the family. "Accordingly," found Gerda L. Schulman, "both the marital alliance and the 'adoption' of the youngest child cut across original family boundaries and represent significant movement toward the becoming of a 'new family.'" In the Krogh household, Julie did not become a mutual favorite.

"I'm jealous of the relationship between Marilyn and Julie," said William, "of the attention they give one another. Marilyn sticks up for Julie too often, and I think she has spoiled the child. Julie is uncomfortable with men—she doesn't really know her father—and so she runs to Marilyn for everything. And Marilyn cuddles her."

"That's true," Marilyn admitted. "Julie was an infant when her father and I divorced. I feel guilty about having separated her from her father, and so I've tried to make it up to her in other ways, probably by overindulging her. You've got to remember, I raised her all by myself. I'm finding it hard to let go."

Michelle, William's youngest, has not been treated to the kind of indulgence that so often falls upon the little ones in a family. There are times she comes very close to accepting Marilyn as her natural mother—she has even called her Mom several times (the other children call their stepparents by first names). Just when Michelle and Marilyn seem closest, Julie hops on her mother's lap —this is her way of saying to Michelle, *This is not your real mother*—and Michelle gets the message and retires to her room. These incidents have occurred less frequently in the past year,

Marilyn and William agree. They feel confident that Michelle and Marilyn are on comfortable ground.

Her mother's abandonment seems to have affected Tania more than it has her sisters. Where Laura was able to direct her energies to running the family, Tania had nothing to run and no one to run to. So she ran with a crowd, became sexually promiscuous, and got into difficulties at school. Marilyn saw Tania as a personal challenge. In the new household, Tania *has* turned over several new leaves. She has also rebelled from time to time. Marilyn takes each setback personally, imposes stern punishments, and sometimes fears she and Tania will permanently lose the ground they had already won.

The issue of discipline, number-one topic in all stephouseholds, is especially controversial in combined families. To which parent do the children look for authority? Whom do they respect? How do the adults regard one another—as parental figures to each other's children or as bystanders? What fits? What is right?

"When it came to discipline, we bounced around a lot," said William. "Marilyn and I had agreed to discuss any situations that arose before we meted out punishment, but it just didn't work out that way. You can't hold a conference every time a child does something that makes you angry. Sometimes, one of us was disciplining the other's child and the parent thought it was too harsh."

"There is a difficult problem in disciplining 'yours' and 'mine,'" Marilyn interjected. "You're very protective of your own children. Many times, I would find myself accusing William, 'Hey, don't you think you're a little harder on my kids than you are on your own?' At one point, we decided each of us would handle our own children. But that doesn't work. In the first place, it's unnatural. In the second, the kids *know* it's unnatural.

"I remember an incident," Marilyn continued. "I was scolding Michelle for something she'd done. Suddenly, I saw this hurt look come over her face and I stopped myself. But then I realized she really did deserve some response from me. So I put my arms around her and told her, firmly, 'Michelle, I love you. That's why I will scold you when you deserve it—because I care.' That felt right to me. Michelle accepted it because it *was* right. Since then, William and I handle the children—it doesn't matter *whose* children—as the need arises. I won't tell you we've overcome our sensitivity to *who* is critical of *whose* children, but we're better able to talk about these reactions calmly, with a lot less suspicion about motives and feelings and favoritism creeping into our discussions."

The question of discipline is so important, further discussion of this controversial subject will be found in Chapter 10.

Stepsibling Relationships in Combined Families

For many children, the announcement that their custodial parent plans to be remarried to someone who also has children and that all are going to live together as one happy family is greeted with as much skepticism as the hesitant swimmer's response to the invitation, "Come on in; the water's fine." Such children are not so sure about the temperature of the water. They aren't even certain they want to swim. Plunk!

As the stepparenting relationship suffers from the myth of instant love, so does the expectation of instant camaraderie place an unreal burden on stepsiblings who need time to get to know one another. The children had no courtship. *They* did not solemnly choose to love and honor one another. Where the adults may be glowing in the pleasure of gaining a loving partner, the children may be struggling with emotions of loss. They now must share the affection of the caretaking parent—not only with a new mate but with other children in the home as well.

"Although sharing, especially of a parent's affection, is a central issue in all sibling rivalry, in the step relationship problems of sharing are intensified," believes psychiatrist Richard A. Gardner. "In the intact home, siblings come along gradually and the child is gradually desensitized to the need to be the sole object of his parents' affection. Over a period of time, the child resigns himself to a certain amount of sharing. In the stepfamily, you have the sudden appearance of the rivals without an opportunity for desensitization."

Countless stepbrothers and stepsisters have grown to like, to respect, and to have great affection for one another. Many others have lived together in hatred. There is, of course, a wide range of emotions in between. How the youngsters interact depends on the personalities of all family members, the differences in age (between child and child, stepparent and child), outside influences on the family (are one set of children indulged by the exiled parent so that all members of the merged family are *obviously* not equal?), even on the sex of the stepsiblings.

(An interesting observation: Lucile Duberman studied reconstituted families and noted that, whereas in the primary family the closer relationships tend to be between siblings of the same sex, in stepfamilies closer relationships develop between stepsiblings of opposite sex. Duberman hypothesizes that this may be a result of sexual attraction that, given the family setting, cannot lead to romance and therefore results in friendship.)

Two Sets of Rules, Two Different Life Styles

So much also depends on how the adults treat the children in the household. There is a strong temptation for a parent to hold up one's own offspring as role models to children who have joined the family. When two different life styles combine, it is natural for the parents to view their own life style, as reflected in their children, as preferred.

Betty, a rather formal divorcée, mother of two sons, who married a widower with two younger children, a daughter and son, felt very strongly about having everyone remain at the dinner table until after the dessert dishes were cleared. During the years following her divorce, when she'd been the only parent in her home, she had turned, more and more, to her teen-age sons for companionship. Dinner hour was the sharing, socializing time of the family's day.

Stephen, Betty's second husband, is a fieldworker for a social welfare agency. His job keeps him on the road a good deal of the time. During his wife's long illness and following her death, Stephen arranged for the children to be cared for by a capable housekeeper. The woman was conscientious about preparing nutritious meals, but she was also pleased to have the children finish dinner quickly and be off to their next activity: doing homework or watching television.

The life styles of the two families clashed. Betty said, "Since Stephen is out of town so often, it falls to me to take on the task of teaching his children family manners." The paradigm of propriety, needless to say, has become *her* younger son. (The older boy is away at college.) It is an honor he has not sought.

What has Betty accomplished? She has bought the enmity of her stepchildren and made it impossible for her son to be accepted by his stepfather's children.

Other, more sensitive women than Betty also raised the difficult matter of merging different life styles. "I still haven't solved this," said one. "You do manage to convey to the stepchildren that 'our values are different,' and you're a saint if you don't indicate, somehow, that yours are better. *In the stepfamily, there's an editorial going on all the time.*"

Can stepsiblings grow to like one another? Yes! For some, especially those who have been only children, stepsiblings can be the sisters and brothers they never had. The remarriage provides peers and companionship. For them, the stepfamily is a good place to be.

Many stepparents interviewed stressed that of all the problems they'd anticipated before the remarriage, the one that didn't emerge as a major issue was that the children of the two families would not get along. (Those who came into the marriage with children of their own had resigned themselves to the fact that siblings squabble.) What was more likely to happen, they discovered, was that the children would unite against a common enemy: the parents.

Sometimes, the presence of other children in the stepfamily can be helpful. In her work with stepfamilies, Gerda L. Schulman observed that:

. . . if a stepchild feels mistreated and neglected by his stepmother or indifferently treated by his stepfather, but he sees similar behavior toward the natural child, the stepchild feels somewhat reassured. He no longer feels that he is hated because he is not the real child, and he can view the stepparent more realistically as a human being with shortcomings. More significantly, because each child in such a family is in the same position, empathy and mutual support develop more easily among the stepsiblings.

There are bound to be clashes in the combined family. In the first-wed family, it takes a while for husband and wife to establish a home that allows for their individual preferences (remember, this is a time of merger, too) and reflects areas of compromise. When children come along, the two adults (now parents) establish family rules as the needs arise. When do the children go to bed? Do family members have dinner together? Are children expected to put away their toys and, later, to keep their rooms neat? What are the duties, the privileges? Is this an informal family? Do the children address their parents or friends of their parents by first names? Do the people in the family wear bathrobes? Is nudity acceptable? What is the family style of discipline? Are the rules clear?

No *one* pattern is right or wrong, so long as the rules are understood by all family participants.

The rules are not clear in combined families. Power struggles are likely to emerge over seemingly insignificant matters, often because the partners are afraid to raise (some even fear to recognize) the larger issues. *Stepfamilies are families at risk.* "You're likely to be more angry with your stepchildren than with your own," said a stepmother, "and so you don't act naturally for fear that so much anger will come out, and so then you take your anger out on your spouse."

Let's look at some of the "small matters" that often loom large in step.

TABLE TALK

Table habits were raised as sources of conflict by an overwhelming number of combined families with whom I spoke. Generally speaking, when the woman had been the caretaking parent, her children were expected to remain at table until the close of the meal. Youngsters in male-headed families, on the other hand, tended to eat and run. This was the situation that Marilyn and William Krogh found in their home.

"Of course it bothered me at first," said Marilyn. "Then I realized that table manners were the *least* of our problems, and I wasn't going to blow them up to create a major issue. So, we told the kids that all children who want dessert have to stay put for it; the others (especially William's dieting daughters) may leave. I like to sit over my coffee, and William keeps me company."

Another difference: Marilyn's children hadn't been required to clear the table or put their own dishes in the sink. William's daughters not only cleared the table in their first home, but were responsible for washing the dishes as well. In the combined household, all children do the dishes (and the vacuuming and the windows), rotating responsibilities according to a posted schedule.

"The word *compromise* is central to most of the advice I have given in step situations—a recognition that the relationships will not be perfect," said Dr. Richard Gardner. "When two families combine, the word *compromise* is the old standby. When I counsel children—especially those who visit but don't reside with the new family—I like the old adage, 'When in Rome, do as the Romans.' It's fine to express yourself, I say, but don't expect the new family to change dramatically for you. I counsel *parents* to ask themselves the questions, 'What's the big deal? Is it worth getting into a power struggle about things that aren't so important?' "

One common mealtime hassle raised by a combined family involves two different ways of looking at life. Their comments follow.

Herb: "It hurts me to see children leave food on their plates. I was brought up to follow the dictate, 'What's on your plate, you eat.' You know, 'The children in Europe are starving.' "

Pam: "I, on the other hand, am convinced the children in Europe are drinking wine with their pasta. I *don't* feel that children have to finish whatever they've been served. I don't even think they have to eat what's been prepared, unless they've requested a special dish and I've cooked it for them. I like to try out different recipes, but if the kids don't want what I've concocted, they may go into the kitchen and make a peanut butter sandwich. The important thing to me is that I don't get up and prepare something else for them. I had no sympathy with Herb's demands that the children—his *and* mine—finish all that was on their plates, and I told him so."

Herb: "That's one of the demands I've dropped. I'm still uncomfortable about seeing food wasted, but I try to keep my mouth shut about it."

FOOD

Disagreements about food may uncode into some very different messages than how rare a hamburger should be. Children often use food as a medium to express their anger. When they reject what has been prepared for them, they are often really rejecting the cook: the stepmother. The children are saying, *"You* are not acceptable."

It is important not to get hung up over the food itself, counsels California family therapist Thelma Kaplan, but to try to get at the deeper issue: what is the hidden agenda here?

She offers a script as an example of how one can respond to challenges with positive communication:

Stepchild: "I don't like your cooking. My mommy's a better cook."

Stepmother: "Oh, I'm sorry you don't like what I've prepared. Perhaps you can come shopping with me and we'll buy some foods you like, or you can help me cook dinner the next time."

It takes a stepmother with very high self-esteem to be able to *not* respond to the challenge that is flung at her, but in the long run it is a better way to respond than to fall into the child's trap of having you engage in competition with the mother (a competition, by the way, that is always going on in the child's mind).

The other side of that dinner plate: it is also possible to be *too* aware, to always be looking for hidden messages. Sometimes, when a child tells you, "I don't like lasagna" (and you have just prepared a sizable casserole of lasagna), the child means no more than what he or she has said. The youngster may eat tomorrow's quiche Lorraine with gusto.

A family therapist suggests, "Don't look for slights. It is possible, even likely, to be ultrasensitive when you are insecure in a relationship. Children argue with their parents all the time. Don't be supersensitive."

PRIVACY

Earlier in this book, privacy (or its absence) was raised as a disturbing issue for the stepfamily in which one partner is new to the whole business of living with children. In combination families, privacy is also a matter of some concern, but the issue comes up differently. At the very least, both parents are by now accustomed to the intrusiveness of children. *How* each family respects the privacy of each of its members takes on a lot of importance. Do the attitudes of the respective families conflict with one an-

other? You ought to find out: do all members of each family
knock on doors before entering bedrooms? Are the children permitted in the parents' bedroom? If there are college-age young
people, how do the grownups in authority feel about permitting
them to invite members of the opposite sex to visit? to share a
room? Can anyone open letters addressed to others in the family?
Are there rules concerning the use of the telephone? (One stepfather found that his wife's children would get on the extension and
relay messages—"Sally's expecting a phone call in five minutes"
—while he was speaking on the phone. Evidently, that sort of behavior had gone unchecked in the children's first family. It was
not to continue in the combined family.) Are parents allowed to
go through the children's drawers, even when the intention is only
to create order out of chaos? All of these issues of privacy were
raised by the combined families who were interviewed. All were
offered as examples of mores that were accepted by the individual
families, but were trouble spots in combination.

The entire subject of *bedtime* emerges as a privacy issue.

For Mary Jane, privacy translated into the evening hours after
nine o'clock. That was the hour when her children were to be in
bed or, as they grew older and their bedtime hours were extended,
at least in their rooms. "I need some time for myself," she declared, "some time when I am not constantly having to deal with
children."

When she met Joe, who had custody of two children, Mary
Jane never thought to raise the question of bedtime. So much else
seemed so much more important. Joe's teen-agers, Mary Jane
soon discovered, were accustomed to staying up until after the
eleven o'clock news and used the evening hours to call upon their
father for help with homework assignments. How could Mary
Jane expect *her* children to go to their rooms when Joe's youngsters were evidently up and about? Moreover, she didn't feel right
about asking her stepchildren to change their habits, when their
own father lived in the home and it was clear that he didn't have
any objection to their presence.

One way to resolve the problem might have been for Mary Jane
to explain her privacy needs to Joe and his children, at the same
time recognizing her stepchildren's wish to involve their father in
their activities. The entire family might have sought a solution

that acknowledged and responded to the needs of all its members. At the time of our interview, however, Mary Jane was still complaining about the frustration she felt; she had not done anything to resolve matters.

Naomi and Mike Clark dealt with a similar conflict constructively. Theirs, too, is a his-and-hers household. Naomi and Mike were in sharp disagreement on the issue of whether children should be seen and heard when their parents entertain guests. Mike adamantly voted no; he expected his three youngsters to greet his friends, then occupy themselves elsewhere in the roomy Tudor house. "My friends haven't left *their* children at home to come spend an evening entertaining mine," he believed.

Naomi has always encouraged her eleven-year-old daughter, Amanda, to join the grownups. She believed this would help the child gain poise and that such get-togethers would expose the young girl to a lot of good ideas. Since her parents' divorce, Amanda spends every other weekend at her father's apartment. Thus she was not even a constant intruder.

The family reached a compromise. Those children who want to may join their parents and their friends for about an hour (nobody watches the clock), after which they're expected to excuse themselves from the gathering. As Amanda grows older, she often elects to spend more time with the other children, which is both a source of delight and some sadness for her mother.

Preparing the Children

The Clarks are rather sophisticated in knowing how to talk together as a family. In addition to the practical experience he has gained as a stepfather, Mike makes his living as a family therapist. Naomi raises bonsai. "I talk to my plants," she says.

When Mike and Naomi agreed to live together (a year before they made the decision to marry), they expected some opposition to the plan from the children. Neither of their former spouses had remarried, and the children still clung to the hope that their parents would kiss and make up. To help them come to grips with their new reality, Naomi and Mike invented a game.

"We paid each child a dime for every statement they could come up with about what they didn't like about the idea of our

living together," described Mike. "They came up with some
doozies, including an expressed reluctance to merge my dog with
Naomi's two cats. Our objective was to get the children to
verbalize their anxieties. It was equally important for us to let
them know this was *not* the most ideal situation and that we'd all
have some adjusting to do."

"My tendency in talking with friends in our situation who seem
supercomplacent (they move in together and they tell me there
are no problems . . . everything's fine and the kids are just
great)," said Naomi, "is to tell them, 'Don't you believe it.
You're just not letting the children know it's okay to speak out.'"

If there is one tenet above all that is crucial to the success of
any family and, therefore, especially so in the stepfamily, it is
this: OPEN COMMUNICATION BETWEEN FAMILY MEM-
BERS IS ESSENTIAL.

A second principle should be worded: DO THINGS ON THE
BASIS OF WHAT IS NATURAL TO YOU. In conversations
with combined families across the nation, several different approaches to dealing with other people's children were discussed.
Of these, three separate patterns became clear. The stepparent responded to the other parent's child by: (1) being scrupulously
"fair"; (2) bending over backward to reassure the stepchild of
her or his acceptance; and (3) favoring one's own offspring.

BEING FAIR

Because this calls for constant assessment of the equities of
each situation and doesn't permit for spontaneous, natural action, this may be the most *unfair* of all approaches.

The speaker is Ruth, a woman in her late thirties: "When my
husband and I combined our families, which included his fourteen-year-old son and my boy, who was thirteen, I found myself
involved in very self-conscious parenting. I was meticulous about
equity. If I bought two pairs of pants for one of the boys who had
outgrown his trousers, I ran out and bought two for the other boy
the very same day. Nobody was going to accuse *me* of favoring
one over the other. I never relaxed, I never dropped my guard.
I felt as if all the adjusting was on my shoulders. My husband
remained uninvolved. I think he believed that family harmony
was woman's work. I think I did, too. We lived in an atmosphere
of accountability and tension."

Ruth and her second husband are divorced. Her son is now seventeen. He does his own shopping.

BENDING OVER BACKWARD

Sometimes you bend over backward to show your husband how close you've grown to his children and, in so doing, hurt your own. You may rely on the so-called natural bond between parent and child to carry you and your natural children through the transitional period of the merger; but if you do so, it's a serious miscalculation. Chances are, your child is as anxious about the remarriage as is your stepchild. He or she has the same kind of fears and doubts about the new situation. At this time, your own child needs strong reassurance from you that he or she *is* special, that your relationship is unique.

At the same time, your stepchild will be more comfortable if you welcome him slowly . . . take it easy . . . and don't overwhelm.

Howard Samuelson, president of Remarrieds, Inc., suggests: "The stepparent must develop a responsible relationship to the youngsters slowly, over the years, just as natural parents do. I think that sometimes stepparents try too hard—they act in a strained or unnatural way. You cannot force a child's affection. When a child has a chance to get used to the idea of having a new father or mother, and when he is sure he is loved for himself, he will begin to warm up. . . . Looking back on my own remarried life, I know that my slow approach to my stepchildren was right."

FAVORING ONE'S OWN CHILDREN

One stepmother made the guilty admission, "I try to be even-handed in the way I treat the kids, but my children are *my* children." Stepparents who realize this is a normal response—that it's okay—can stop thinking about guilt and go on to work on the new relationships.

In *The Parents' Book About Divorce*, Richard Gardner addresses this clearly:

> Parents who believe that they should be just as loving toward their stepchildren as they are toward their own children are placing an unnecessary burden upon themselves and will inevitably feel guilty about not living up to this unrealistic standard.

I am not claiming that it is not *possible* for a stepparent to love a stepchild as much as his or her own; I am only saying that it is entirely reasonable that he or she may not. There are stepparents who, although they do feel a preference for their natural children, consider that it would be harmful to the stepchildren if they were to reveal this to them. "They're all the same to me," they profess. "Sometimes, I forget which ones are mine, which ones theirs, and which ones ours." I find such "forgetfulness" incredible and so, I believe, do the children involved. Such a stepparent would do better to relate to the stepchildren, at the proper time and in the appropriate situation, comments along these lines: "Yes, I do love my own children more than I love you. I have known them much longer and there has been more time for our love to grow. I do feel great affection for you children and I hope that as time goes on I will feel even more. The more loving things we do for one another, the more our love should grow. And that's the same with my children as well."

A suggestion: reread that advice as if it were addressed to the stepchild. Suppose that it begins: *"Children* who believe they should be just as loving toward their *stepparent* as they are toward their own parent are placing an unnecessary burden upon themselves and will inevitably feel guilty about not living up to this unrealistic standard. . . ." The message? It is best for *all* parties in the combined family to take matters slowly, to use the crock pot instead of the pressure cooker, and not to aim for a perfect blend but rather to recognize the pleasures to be enjoyed in retaining some of the distinct flavors of the separate ingredients.

TIME TOGETHER ALONE

"When people come together in stepfamilies, there is a great emphasis on fusion, on recreating the nuclear family," observed Judith, a young graduate student who'd been raised, since the age of ten, in a his-and-hers family. "That attitude, which sounds reasonable, is in fact harmful. It doesn't show sufficient respect for individual relationships. Each stepparent should respect her spouse's relationship with his own children and allow them the time they must have together, and the natural parent must not deny the specialness of that relationship."

It is a good idea for members of combined families to break up those combinations once in a while. Parents would do well to arrange some time alone with their own children, for a week, for a weekend, or at the least for an afternoon, to reinforce those primary commitments. Every stepparent also ought to put aside time to be alone with his or her stepchildren, for them to get to know one another better, to build their relationships. And each husband and wife should step away from the entire family every once in a while, for a week, for a weekend, or at the least for an afternoon or evening, to strengthen their commitment to one another—and to maintain their sanity.

5

Living with One Set of Children

Suppose husband and wife each have children from a previous marriage. In the usual remarriage situation, the woman's children move in with the newly wed couple; the man's offspring continue to reside with *their* mother. They visit their father at his home according to an arranged schedule.

The *semiblended family* presents a unique challenge to the noncustodial parent: how to live with other people's children when you no longer make your home with your own.

PLEADING GUILTY

The first (indeed the overriding) issue the exiled parent must come to grips with is his guilt. Addressing "The Common Problems of Stepparents and Their Spouses" in the *American Journal of Orthopsychiatry,* Drs. Emily and John Visher noted:

> Sometimes, the feelings of guilt are so strong that the stepfather is unable to enjoy his stepchildren. He cannot give freely and openly to the stepchildren with whom he lives because of his guilt at depriving his natural children of fatherly affection and concern. In extreme cases, the stepfather may develop strong resentments and antagonisms toward his stepchildren, and there may be a complete inhibition of warmth and love towards them.
> . . . When a group of stepfathers met recently, guilt was the predominant theme of the discussion.

Somewhat tense, Sheldon was quick to explain why he'd phoned me and asked to be interviewed. "I want *someone* to write that men are as sensitive, caring, concerned, and loving with regard to their children as are women," he said. "It's true, the man may be the one who moves out of the home, but he doesn't do so lightly. I care terribly about not living with my daughter. I know the pain will always be there.

"If you go on to marry someone who has children, as I did," Sheldon continued, "and those children live with you, and it's *their* voices you hear every evening when you come home from work (not your own child's welcoming greeting), the pain is reinforced. I feel a need to prove I *can* be a good husband and father, but when I help my stepchildren with their homework, for example, I find myself wondering: *who's there to help my daughter with her arithmetic problems?* My ex-wife is lousy at math. . . .

"And I find that I romanticize what living with my own child was like. I remember the good moments and forget the times I was angry with my daughter, her way of whining that got on my nerves, the times I wished she would leave me alone for a while. In memory, she was never bad, and in comparison my stepchildren seem noisy or intrusive. Sometimes, I take my resentment out on my wife's children, simply because they're there. I'm brusque with them when they don't deserve it. When I stop to think about *that*, I have a different kind of guilt to deal with. . . ."

"Many men have anger about the inequities of this kind of setup," agrees psychologist Nina Cohen, "and that anger often keeps them from making a full commitment to the stepchildren with whom they live."

BUILDING A WALL

Fred chose to make no commitment to his new stepchildren. So great was his guilt at living apart from his own four youngsters, Fred managed to remove himself completely from any association with the son and daughter of his second wife, Harriet, even though they all lived together in a house that, to the visitor, seemed as warm and welcoming as the down-filled pillows scattered about the family room.

Following dinner each evening, Harriet's eleven-year-old son, Robert, would go directly to his room and turn his radio on at full volume. The boy, who was devoted to his own father, was furious with his mother for remarrying. He took his anger out on everyone who touched his life. Robert needed help.

"Fred's way of dealing with Robert was to not get involved," said Harriet. "He made his position clear: Robert was not his son."

Dinner over, Fred made a beeline for the den where he could be alone with *his* misery. And there sat Harriet and her daughter, every evening, in the living room, looking at one another. . . .

Alternate weekends, Fred's youngsters came for a visit—always all four of them, always as a group. Sometimes, Harriet's children would be out of town visiting *their* father. Said Harriet, "We lived with a revolving door. One group would exit as the second group entered." Sometimes, Harriet's son and daughter would be at home when Fred's children filed in, but the two separate family groups remained just that.

"They were horrible weekends," said Harriet. "I did all the work. My children disappeared, and Fred's children expected to be treated as guests. Fred didn't deal with that because he had his kids for such a short time, he didn't want to spend any part of it as a disciplinarian. After his children were returned home, Fred and I always wound up the weekend by having a terrible fight."

At long last (it was a matter of months that seemed forever), a family therapist was consulted. She felt strongly that Fred could no longer ignore Robert. He *had to relate* to Harriet's children, even if that relationship was going to be expressed primarily by discipline—for it was clear that Robert needed someone to take him in hand, to set some rules and some guidelines for his behavior. "You have to care about someone to fight with him," the counselor told Fred.

A year ago, Robert solved the problem in his own way. He picked up and moved into his father's home.

Now it is Harriet who finds herself struggling with feelings of guilt. "I feel terrible about not having my son live with me," she confessed. "It's a harsh way to gain understanding, but I think I've come to have a better feeling for what Fred was trying to come to grips with. I should have been more understanding of his anguish and tried to help him deal with it rather than constantly accusing him of not caring. I think he was afraid to form a new attachment to a child, saw it as betrayal of his own children, and here I was —nagging him on. In a way, my son and my husband were two sides of the same coin. Each was working out the guilt of having 'abandoned' someone each loved.

"When Robert left to live with his father," Harriet continued, "I went into a six months' depression. I felt so guilty. I often thought . . . if I'd worked harder at my first marriage, this wouldn't have happened. My son would be living with me. But I couldn't go back and replay that tape, so I resolved that I'd direct my efforts to keeping up a relationship with my son. Once a month, I check in at a hotel in the city where Robert now lives, and we visit. I take him out to breakfast. If he's playing in a baseball game, you'll find me in the stands. If he has other plans, I let him know where I'll be and that he can work me into his day at his convenience. I'm persistent. Sometimes, Robert grows angry with me, but I'm not going to let him shut the door on me. He knows I love him, that I always will welcome him back."

Children of divorce, like Robert, often handle their confusion by running away from home, for they know there is another home they can run *to*. Custody agreements set at the time of separation are not sealed in stone. This is not necessarily a bad thing for children, so long as both parents are not constantly wooing them, encouraging them to choose (time and again) between one parent and family and the other. Children should know that the doors to their parents' homes are open to them. A revolving door, however, is not recommended. Parent and child are likely to find themselves trapped in the continuous motion.

BREAKING DOWN A WALL

Since Robert moved to his father's home, Harriet has taken the time and made the effort to come to know her stepchildren. Is it a coincidence that the one child of the four to whom she feels closest is Fred's son Randy, who is next in age to Robert?

Encouraged by her interest, Randy has been able to help Harriet understand what *his* feelings were like during early visits to his father's new home shortly after the remarriage had taken place. "This was your house, not ours," Randy explained, "and my sisters and brother and I resented that. Your kids lived here with our father; we did not. I never was comfortable here. I felt that you and your children were judging us. We couldn't just be ourselves. I was just waiting to hear your children call my father Daddy. *That* would have driven me up the wall."

Harriet in turn confided that she'd never cared what her children called their stepfather nor how she was addressed by her stepchildren. She just wished each would *acknowledge* the other in a friendly manner. "*You* would have been driven up a wall," she repeated Randy's words. "I think we'd all have been better off if we hadn't allowed a wall to be erected in the first place."

RESIDENTS VERSUS INTRUDERS

In combined families, there is a tendency for one of the groups to become dominant, the family whose rules obtain, the one that sets the tone while the other family assumes a secondary role. *In the semiblended family, the difference between the two units is more apparent* and will take longer to resolve because several participants (the nonresident children) come and go, underscoring their relationship to the rest of the family: they are the visitors.

The change in the household is confusing to the live-in youngsters, too.

Sally and Joel have been living together for four years, the last two as husband and wife. Sally's daughters, Claudine, ten, and Debra, five, live with the couple in a stylish brownstone in Brooklyn's Park Slope district. Joel's only son, Graham, eleven, lives nearby, making it easy for him to visit his father every weekend. He also comes by for dinner, and sometimes stays overnight on Tuesdays. Everybody, it seems, gets along well with everyone else. And yet . . .

"Debby is a very cuddly little girl," says her mother. Joel nods agreement. "She'd really like to be very close to Joel. During the time we've lived together, I've watched Joel loosen up and respond to her. It's pretty hard for him not to. Debby will climb on Joel's lap when he reads her a bedtime story. They're really quite wonderful together. Then it's Tuesday night and Graham comes by. Immediately, Joel switches currents with Debby, from hot to cold. Debby draws near him in a way that is natural for her, and Joel moves away. Debby doesn't know what to make of it."

"I feel guilty displaying any affection for my stepchildren when my own son's around," Joel explained. "It feels somehow . . . indecent. How can I put it?" He searches for a comparison, and finds one. "It's like having extramarital sex in front of your wife."

"Debby doesn't understand her stepfather's mood changes," said Sally. "I do, but that doesn't help Debby.

"On the other hand," Sally continued, "Joel's son, Graham, and I have a nice, easygoing relationship, now that I've faced the fact that he's not going to accept me as a mother. When I pressed for that role, early on (I was looking forward to having a son), Graham backed off. He already has a mother. But now he and I are friends. Still, I find I'm self-conscious with him. At times when I'd like to move toward him, I notice one or the other of my daughters being hypervigilant, taking note of my every move. Immediately, what was intended to be a hug is abridged to an affectionate pat. We probably would have resolved this sooner if we all lived together. The fact that Graham does have another home (as do my daughters, but they visit their father less often than Graham sees Joel) has worked to maintain some of the barriers I'd like to have seen tumble."

Every once in a while, an incident reminds Joel and Sally that they're still vulnerable where their own children are concerned. Such was the incident of the chocolate cupcake. It is hard for the couple to retell the story without smiling at the pettiness of it all but, they stress, that's what convinced them they were dealing with a serious matter.

There was, it seems, one chocolate cupcake in the house. Claudine wanted it. So did Graham. Joel, who was at home, awarded the cupcake to his son. When Sally came home from work, Claudine met her at the door with the tale of this injustice. Claudine said she thought the cupcake should have been divided between her and her stepbrother, and her mother agreed. Later, in the privacy of their room, Sally confronted Joel. He responded with a vehemence that surprised them both.

"Why should Graham have to share again?" Joel shouted. "It's enough that he has to share *me!* The very least I could do for my kid was to give him the damn cupcake!"

"You ask about blending?" Sally responded to my question. "I'm afraid there's still too much polarization. Our individual children still view their own parent in this house as the primary parent, and I'll tell you a story that illustrates how guilty we grownups are of the same assessments.

"One Friday, Graham was due at our home at one o'clock. Well, I came home at about three, expecting to find Graham here —but the place was empty. I waited. The hands on the clock passed four . . . still, no Graham. I was really worried. I phoned Joel at his office. Quite casually, he told me Graham had called earlier, at about noon, for permission to stay awhile after school for a game of soccer with some of his friends.

" 'But why didn't you call home and tell *me?'* I asked. Joel was abashed. He'd simply never thought it was important. Father and son had communicated, and that was enough. If it had been Claudine who'd phoned, Joel would have got in touch with me and relayed the message because, very simply, Claudine's *my* child.

"But Joel's not the only one who sees the children in relation to who's the parent," said Sally. "When I do call upon his services on behalf of my children, I try to keep requests to a minimum. I'll ask if he'll *please* drive one of the girls to her music lesson. I always phrase each need as a request. I say please and thank you a lot. If I were dealing with the girls' real father, I'd simply *tell* him the children had to be driven somewhere and whichever one of us was free would be *expected* to do it."

"There *is* a difference in my being part of a semiblended family," said Joel, "and it is this. I think of myself as head of this household. In my first marriage, I was head of the family."

THE LONELINESS OF THE LONG-DISTANCE PARENT

Acknowledging its limitations, many men who no longer live with their own children find the position of head of a household (even a semiblended one) very attractive. To put it in basic terms, they miss family life. In contrast to the popular portrait of the divorced father as a young-to-middle-aged man about town, divested of responsibility and hell-bent for pleasure, many of the men who spoke with me told of making a difficult adjustment to living alone.

"I had a terrible time coming to grips with the change of position," recalled Tom, whose first marriage broke up after seventeen years and five children. "First, there was the guilt. Then there was the loss of status. I'd been a father, a homeowner, chairman of our school board, a respected member of the community. Suddenly I found myself living alone in a dingy, cramped apartment that did not have enough room to allow any of the children to stay overnight. I was very lonely, dishonored, and struggling for my own survival.

"When I met Stacy," he continued, "I was glad she had three children. I liked the idea of living in an active home again. I also felt she had the kind of parenting experience that would enable her to accept and deal with my children. I was right. Stacy didn't have to marry to become a mother, and so she isn't disappointed when my children don't look to her as one. She understands young people and the stages they go through, and has offered her understanding to my children. Some of them have been willing to accept it.

"You've heard of people having children for the sake of the marriage? Well, Stacy and I were married for the sake of the children. Between us, there were eight young people to consider. There's a tax penalty for marriage, but we went ahead with it. I've never been sorry."

Derek works a few offices down the hall from Tom in a large engineering firm. The two men had not been especially friendly with one another until Derek separated from his first wife and moved out of the comfortable house that has remained home to his ex-wife and his son and two daughters. During working hours, Tom gave Derek a lot of much-needed moral support. He knew very well the pain of transition. Every evening, however, Derek was left to face the solitude of temporary quarters: a spare room sublet from another divorced father. "And I missed the notes on the refrigerator door," said Derek.

Of his recent marriage to Carole, mother of three, Derek commented, "I was ready to move in with a family. I missed the regimen. I also liked the way Carole handled her kids."

Derek and Carole have been married less than a year. "Everything is brand-new to me," said Derek. "The experience of stepparenting has been one of anxiety. The hardest task, as I see it, is trying to fit into a role and maintain my identity. I am Derek, husband, ex-husband, father, stepfather, son-in-law, former son-in-law, brother-in-law, former brother-in-law, and so on. Sometimes it's hard for me to figure out who I really am, I'm trying so hard to live up to the expectations of all those titles."

While Derek is working on fitting comfortably into his new family, he is also working out the problems of relationships to his first family. He is fighting for custody of his thirteen-year-old son Scott.

"I was one of the people who was going to have a civilized, intelligent divorce," he explained. "There were going to be no strict rules on visitation. My ex-wife and I live a half hour's distance from each other, so there was no commuting problem. The schedule was to be up to the children. I didn't want them to interrupt their plans because they *had* to be at Daddy's home. Two of the children are teen-agers, and they lead pretty busy lives. I wanted to respect their schedules and to let them know I was there for them when they wanted and needed me.

"I found instead that visits were being used by their mother as reward and punishment: *If you don't clean your room, you won't be allowed to see your father.* At one point, I was laid off from a job and had to reduce my support payments. Now it was I who was being punished. My ex-wife would permit me to see the kids only for three hours a week until I'd caught up on my financial obligations."

HOW TO LIVE WITH A SPOUSE WHO NO LONGER LIVES WITH HIS CHILDREN

All the while Derek has been talking, his wife, Carole, has been sitting calmly, listening, nodding now and then. This has been Derek's story.

Carole is a young woman, twelve years her husband's junior,

the kind of woman whose appearance calls forth the adjectives "cute" and "pert." She is much more solid a person than those descriptions imply. Now Carole speaks up.

"Everyone talks about the pain of the parent who does *not* live with his children," she says, "and it's real, but few people realize the terrible strain this places on the person whose children do live in the home. I ache for Derek. Every time his ex-wife does something to separate him from his children, I feel his pain. He becomes withdrawn, and there's no way to reach him.

"I feel guilty because I've managed to keep my children. I find myself watching them more carefully: are they making too much noise? Are they pestering Derek? I try to intervene when I see them getting on his nerves. I know Derek will have to work out his own relationship with my children, but I feel I have an obligation not to impose them on him. I believe I'd be a lot less guilty if the deal were more equal, if *I* had to cope with my stepchildren day in and day out. Oh, I'd feel a lot of other emotions, I know, but one of them would *not* be guilt."

Carole is not simply speaking hypothetically. She is supportive of Derek in his action to obtain custody of Scott. Her support, however, is not without reservation. In principle, she recognizes Derek's right to have his children under his roof, but reality finds Carole anxious about what seems to be a real possibility of living full time with Scott. One of her fears is that Scott will replace eleven-year-old Sandy, Carole's son, as oldest child in the family —a treasured status. Another consideration is that Sandy and his stepfather "just don't get along." For Derek's son to join the family now, Carole worries, would add one more obstacle to the establishment of a satisfactory relationship between Derek and her own son.

In favor of the arrangement is the fact that Carole and her stepson, Scott, do like one another. They get along. Carole sees herself as a surrogate mother to Derek's children. "I am not an adoptive mother," she says, "but I hope the children see me as someone who cares about them and for them—as a friend, a teacher, a respected adult."

This was not the first time I heard a stepparent refer to herself as a surrogate parent. For those who accept this role, it can offer rewards for adult and for child.

"I find it easier to be a surrogate than to be a parent," claimed a partner in a semimerged family, a man who has functioned in both roles. "My own adolescent children and I have had a terrible time as they've struggled to break away and I've struggled to hold on. As a surrogate parent, I have found my stepchildren don't have a similar need to throw me off, nor I to hold fast. They are *not* my children. Thus, they have been able to become my friends."

6

The Visitors, or Weekend Family

Having identified the guilt of the parent who no longer lives with his or her children, let us now take several looks at what happens in some stepfamilies when the "abandoned children" arrive for a visit.

Schedules vary widely. Overnight bag in hand, some youngsters descend upon the household each and every weekend. Others who live at a distance and cannot make frequent trips from one parent's home to the other's will spend fewer but longer periods (Christmas, Easter, and summer vacations) with the exiled parent and his or her new family. Some come as seldom as once in several years.

Whichever schedule you arrive at, know that the tempo and tone of life in the visited household is likely to change even before the youngster steps across the threshold of your home and sets the bags down. Visitation has been referred to as a pain-and-pleasure arrangement. It is that.

HOW THE PARENT FEELS

For the parent, the anticipation of seeing one's children is coupled with tension at having to condense the experiences of a week, two weeks, a month, into a span of an evening, a day, forty-eight hours. The parent is concerned that the time spent with his or her children be pleasant; the parent wants the visit to be "meaningful." Much like the working mother, the noncustodial father clings to the hope that the quality of the time he spends with his children will make up for the absence of a quantity of shared experience. Where there are several children, this task is all the more difficult.

A remarried father remarked: "For me, looking forward to seeing my daughters, who are eleven and fifteen, is very much like the excitement I used to feel about dating: making arrangements to see someone I like; anticipating our getting together; going out to dinner. . . . But the time constraints are really difficult, balancing my needs against the children's needs. When the girls come to stay at my home for a weekend, I also have my wife's needs to consider—how much time can I give her, where does she fit in . . . ?"

It is also hard on the noncustodial parent (typically, this is the father) to accept that he will have less influence on his children's lives than would likely have been the case had the primary family remained intact. This helplessness is underscored by Emily Visher, Ph.D., and John Visher, M.D. In their article "The Common Problems of Stepparents and Their Spouses," the authors gainsay the myth that stepchildren are easier when not living in the home. As an example, they cite the situation of a young girl named Pam, who had become a behavior problem.

"If Pam is living with her father and stepmother, day after day," they write,

> the couple may struggle together (and often not so together) to deal with Pam's behavior in a constructive way. . . . If Pam only visits with her father and stepmother, there is even less control and cohesiveness than if Pam lives with them. Since the household where the stepchild visits is one with considerably less control, Pam's father and stepmother may feel completely overwhelmed and helpless in their attempts to deal with her upsetting behavior. . . .

The parent who plays host to his own offspring finds it difficult to accept the downgrading of his role in the lives of those children.

Said one man, "I feel more like a doting uncle to my children than I do like a father. It's not a natural relationship. It's been hard, but I've finally faced the fact that I'm not involved in their day-to-day activities, and so I can't expect to be effective. I can't make sure that they practice their piano lessons. I can't help them with math every other weekend and believe that will do it. You can't know the details of a child's life when you don't live with that child, or make the kind of small talk that is an accepted and important part of a warm and close relationship. It's hard to be casual when every moment counts."

HOW THE CHILD FEELS

Preparing to visit the noncustodial parent, children too build fantasies of what their shared time will be like. Father may have been a stern disciplinarian, a man more involved in the pursuit of pleasure or of business than in the life of the family, but distance has him pictured as loving, understanding. . . . Father may have been concerned and caring, a man who took his place at the head of the table, but the rancor of the parent with whom the child lives may have him pictured as a rotter, a ladies' man, someone who placed his own pleasure before the good of the family.

How the child feels often is a reflection of how the custodial parent regards the divorce and the relationship of former spouse to present partner. Dr. Richard Gardner has observed that "the success of the visit often depends on the behind-the-scenes operations of the non-present parent." A typical situation will have the father remarrying, the mother remaining alone. The natural mother is threatened by the other woman taking over the mother role. She conveys her feelings of distrust to the children who then find themselves in the midst of a conflict of loyalty. If they like their stepmother, aren't they being disloyal to their mother?

How do the children feel when they visit a remarried parent? Expectant, confused—and guilty. Where several youngsters are involved, each also feels competitive. Sibling rivalries, which exist in all families, are intensified during visits to a remarried parent. Each of the children vies for the attention of the visited father.

HOW THE STEPMOTHER FEELS

Where the noncustodial parent is reduced to "doting uncle," the role of stepmother is further removed from that of mother. Dr. Gardner finds that, generally, stepmothers want to please their husbands (if only for self-serving reasons) and to form benevolent relationships with the children. Suppose their efforts at friendship meet with rejection. What are they to do?

Gardner's key word, *compromise,* comes up again. Says the psychiatrist, "The stepmother should compromise her goals (she should lower her sights and not try to be a second mother to the children), but she should not compromise her actions. She can still be warm and motherlike, if that's her style." She need not be, if it is not.

"Four years ago, when John and I married, I really was excited about the prospect of mothering," said Teresa, whose marriage to John is her first. "It was part of a whole romance I'd created. In one ceremony, I would become a wife *and* a mother. . . . John's children, just entering their teens, would come to me with their problems. I would offer a sympathetic ear. . . . We'd have big Sunday breakfasts. . . . Life was to be a Hallmark Christmas.

"Reality has shown itself to be quite the opposite," she declared. "We are *not* a family. The children are visitors—sometimes not even willing visitors—and they have come not to see me but to spend time with their father. I'm in the way. I feel unneeded and unwanted, and I can't wait for them to go so that I can reclaim my home."

The stronger sentiment that generally remains unspoken is: *I can't wait to reclaim my husband.* The visit serves to bring feelings of rivalry much closer to the surface as wife and child test the allegiance of the man who has ties to them both. They want to know, which one of us does he love better?

When the children live with the stepparent, such rivalries are likely to be resolved more quickly than when contacts are occasional and the conflicts are drawn out.

Teresa is jealous, too, of John's continuing relationship with his former wife, a relationship that likely would not have continued had there not been children involved, and she is jealous because she is often excluded from their discussions. "I feel all of our vacations, weekends, and activities are decided in phone conversations between my husband and his ex, as they draw up a schedule of *who* will have the children and *when,*" she said. "I'm expected to accept pleasantly whatever they come up with. Me? I'm to be grateful. After all, I got the man!"

THE VISITORS MEET THE HOME TEAM AND IT'S A WHOLE NEW
GAME

Where husband and wife have children of former marriages and
the offspring of one partner permanently reside with the couple,
the arrival of a second family can be unsettling. This may be true,
quite literally, if the home isn't large enough to house the ex-
panded group comfortably. It is not unusual for the live-in children to vacate their rooms and resettle in makeshift arrangements
in order to make room for the guests. In actuality, physical displacement is less distressing than the other kind of displacement
that is experienced by the home team. That is the displacement of
the attention and affection of the heads of the household onto the
other children who may be viewed, by the children permanently
in the home, as intruders.

"We'd finally reached a point where my girls had kind of accepted Don as a father figure," said a mother whose daughters
make their home with her and their stepfather. "That's true for
Monday and Tuesday. On Wednesday, Michael (Don's *real*
child) comes to stay over and there is terrible jealousy all around.

"Michael arrives 'hyper,' as he tries to find his spot in the
household, to assert that he belongs here, too. My daughters
haven't yet figured out how to take this whirlwind of a boy. More
important, they see their stepfather direct *all* his attention—suddenly—to his son, and they don't know what to make of that either." (Michael's turbulent actions are not at all unusual for the
visiting child who walks into the host home wondering what has
gone on in his absence, and who must also resolve: where do I fit
in?)

YOUTHS BEARING MESSAGES

Dr. Fitzhugh Dodson has called the children of divorce "Shuttle
Kids." It is an apt term. Back and forth from one home to another
they go, often bearing messages.

Twelve-year-old Sandy arrives at her father's home. She carries
a list of demands: "Mom says to tell you the check was late again
and she had to buy on credit from the grocer. . . . The orthodontist says I need braces, but Mom doesn't have the money to
pay for them. . . ."

Two days pass and Sandy returns to her mother: "Dad says if you got rid of the housekeeper, we could afford to pay for orthodontics. . . . Dad tried to call you to explain about the check, but you weren't home. Dad thinks you spend too many nights out during the week."

"Oh, he does. Well, you can tell your father that what *I* do with *my* time is *my* business. He isn't married to me anymore, you know. I'll bet he doesn't tell his new wife what to do . . . *does* he?"

So it goes.

The messages can be more subtle. "I always send my kids to their father's home in torn jeans," admitted one mother. "I hope he and his wife *will* be embarrassed about how the children look. Maybe then they'll go out and buy the kids some clothing for a change. But I doubt it."

This kind of communication need not be related to real financial need. In *Haywire*, the story of her growing-up years, Brooke Hayward (daughter of actress Margaret Sullavan and agent-producer Leland Hayward) describes a typical visit, with her sister, to their father's home, and records her father's harangue: "'I wish to hell [your mother would] buy you some decent clothes. Whenever you come to see me, you're all wearing the worst-looking rags. I'm sure she sends you off like that deliberately. She knows I'll have to outfit you from top to bottom before I can set foot on the street with you.'

"This was true," Brooke Hayward noted. "We always came back from our infrequent visits together with a new wardrobe. . . ."

"Get this across loud and clear," says Dena Whitebook, who is no stranger to the world of Hollywood and Beverly Hills. The associate director of the American Institute of Family Relations (located on Sunset Boulevard in Los Angeles) is adamant. "YOU DO NOT USE THE CHILDREN AS MESSAGE TAKERS," she declares.

It may be tempting—to either parent—but in the long run all who are involved will benefit by having the children feel comfortable in either parent's home. For it is to be expected that the visiting child *will* start out by feeling uncomfortable. Brooke Hayward recalls, "We also had a stepsister, Kitty . . . a pretty child about nine years younger than I. She adored Father and, for a while, changed her name to Kitty Hayward. Although we were very fond of Kitty, we envied her the life we would have liked: a beautiful, chic, smart, funny, doting mother married to, of all people, our father. By comparison we felt unlucky, and we couldn't help making comparisons."

WATCH OUT FOR BOOBY TRAPS

The children are ill at ease with the new liaison. They're torn by loyalties to two parents and they feel hostility toward the stepparent whom they see as having replaced one of their parents in the affection of the other. At the outset of a new relationship, the adults involved should not expect visits from the children to be times of sweetness and light. That may come in time, but stepparents who look for warmth or even hope to hear "please" and "thank you" will meet with disappointment.

Recognize that your partner's children are bound to be distrustful. If they find themselves beginning to like you, they will work to negate those feelings. They may set up confrontations.

Fourteen-year-old Nancy comes down to breakfast in her father's house wearing a dress that is very revealing of her developing figure.

Her stepmother rises to the bait. "Where on earth did you get that?" she blurts out. "You don't mean to tell me you're going to walk down the street in *that* thing."

"My mother bought it for me," Nancy replies. *Zonk.*

Gloria Hull has spent several hours in the kitchen preparing chicken cacciatore for Eric, her seventeen-year-old stepson. He had once mentioned it was his favorite dish.

The family sits down to dinner. "But I've been a vegetarian for the past two months," Eric announces. "I can't eat this. I'm *sure* I must have told you." *Zonk.*

The stepparent who can minimize the effects of the booby traps set by guilt-ridden and confused children will outlast the war and perhaps be able to attain a comfortable truce.

When Gloria (stepmother to the vegetarian) met Arthur Hull (Eric's father), he was going through a very bitter divorce from a woman who had been in and out of mental hospitals for many of the fourteen years of their marriage. "My ex-wife's illness kept me tied to her long after there ceased to be any affection between us," said Arthur, a gentle man. "Even when she was released and came home, I continued to take a lot of abuse from her because of my concern for our son, Eric. On my forty-fifth birthday, she caused a terrible scene. She threw a lamp right at me, and accused me of being involved with somebody else—which wasn't true. The timing of that incident led to my resolve to live my life in my own best interests. Whatever years remained to me, I decided, were going to be as happy as I could make them. I walked out of the house."

It took two years for the divorce, during which time Arthur met and moved in with Gloria, a divorcée and mother of three sons. Two are now away at college. The youngest, Matthew, is thirteen and lives at home. When the divorce became final, Arthur and Gloria married.

After the marriage it was two years before Eric agreed to meet Gloria or to see his father.

"His mother so poisoned Eric's thoughts against me, he refused to have anything to do with me," said Arthur. "God knows *what* she told him about Gloria." Through intermediaries, Arthur kept the door open, and one day Eric walked in. He came, he declared, to tell his father what he thought of him.

It was a beginning. From time to time thereafter, Eric dropped in on the family. "I felt he came as a spy to see how we lived, what we were doing, and so on," said Gloria. "I was extremely discomfited by his visits. What would he go home and report? And I was right. If Eric came for a weekend and saw a new stereo, by Monday evening we'd get a phone call from his mother. 'If you can afford music, you can afford to send me more money,' she'd shout and then she'd hang up.

"Eric also was confused by what went on here," Gloria added. "He'd never seen his father romantically valued before. We do a lot of touching in this house. Eric didn't know how to deal with that. He began to recognize that he'd have to change some of his ideas about people and what was appropriate behavior. He was a very rigid young man.

"Then Eric began to like me," Gloria added, "and he was so torn. He'd start to come close, to talk to me, and then he'd pull back. I'd touch him and he'd jump. His best relationship has always been with my son, Matthew. Whenever Eric visits us, he has to find some place for himself. Being with Matthew seems easiest. The two boys spend a lot of time together."

Eric visits his father's home often now, still generally without prior warning, but sometimes for as long as two weeks at a time. "Our relationship has improved tremendously," Gloria said, "but I'm still consciously always working at having him feel welcome, and so I keep a lot of what I feel inside. I don't *say*, 'Eric, you mess up the room and make a lot of work for me.' But I do *think* it. I'm afraid that if I criticize him, I may lose some of the ground I've gained."

Guest or Member of the Family?

Beverly's son, Adam, fifteen, lives in a duplex apartment with his mother and her third husband, Edward. Marcus, Edward's son, is also fifteen. He lives with his mother and *her* husband in London, England, and sees his father once (sometimes two times) a year.

"When Marcus comes to visit," explained Beverly, "he's a guest. That's how I treat him. For example, I pick up more after him than I do after Adam, who is responsible for his own things. Similarly, I think I allow more mouth and sass out of my stepchild than I do from my own son. I figure we see Marcus so seldom, why use up energy setting down rules."

Leslie: "My stepdaughter, Janice, joins my children and her father at our cottage on Cape Cod every summer. She stays for a month. I'm uncomfortable about setting up visitor's rules. I don't allow my children to chew gum. Janice chews constantly. Now I know that's become a habit, but it irks me—and it's not fair for me to allow Janice to chew and prohibit my children from doing it. But I worry—is it fair to Janice to impose my rules on her and is it worth applying pressure when she'll be going home to her old habits as soon as vacation's over?"

Where does the visiting child fit in? Is the youngster to be treated as a guest or member of the family? The answer for each family will depend on a number of variables: how often the child visits; whether or not other children are part of the household; the temperaments of the adults and the children; the degree of self-esteem of the heads of the household, especially of the stepparent; and the importance they attach to rules and regulations.

One stepmother complained that the table manners of her husband's nine-year-old daughter were atrocious. "She doesn't even unfold her napkin on her lap when we sit down to dinner," this woman said. "It goes downhill from there."

Gloria Hull, on the other hand, is bothered by having to straighten Eric's room, but she has decided it is less important an issue—at this time—than establishing good relations with her husband's son, and so she holds back.

Holding back *over a period of time* helps no one. It contributes to a continuation of the situation in which visiting children feel themselves to be outsiders, and the caretakers of the inn (especially the one who is not their parent) feel themselves ill used. ("What am I doing, waiting on this child hand and foot? What's more, why isn't anybody grateful?")

The distinction between making a fuss about nonimportant matters (unfolded napkins, unless they are a symbol of general rudeness, would fall under this category) and basic co-operation ("In this house, those who do not cook do wash the dishes") is important. Eventually, families who live in combination manage to work out some rules of the house (see Chapter 10). Where family members do not live together, the visiting child may seem always to be on holiday; the hosts (both the natural and the acquired parent) may be using their party manners, and—underlying the festivities—resentments build up. Watch out—the party may be over with a bang!

Mary: "The first year we were married, Richard's three children arrived at our house each and every weekend. We lived in the same town as did Richard's ex-wife. Then, when we moved to

Maine, it became financially impossible for us to have the trio shuttled back and forth. Also, the children were growing older and had their own social lives. They weren't so anxious to pick up and come see us. They did come up every five weeks, however, and *always* as a group.

"Those were horrible weekends. It bothered Richard that I used to say, 'Hey, how about cleaning up.' What right had I to make demands on his poor, abandoned children! Sarah, his daughter, and my son, David (who took his cue from what was going on about him), would just get up from the dinner table and disappear. How could I reprimand my son when everybody else in the place marched to the tune of his or her very own drummer! Richard's two older children disappeared even *before* dessert was served. *I did not like being a maid.* Richard refused to deal with it. He had his kids for such a short time, he refused to assume the role of disciplinarian.

"One day, I looked about the house: at five unmade beds, three stacks of dishes, a full hamper of underwear and socks, and a husband who spent his time doting—but not on me. Systematically, I broke every one of the first stack of dishes. I made quite a scene. Richard came in and we had a fight that deserves to go down in the annals of remarriages. We're separated now. I'm convinced Santa Claus is a divorced father!"

Coming Home

When Santa Claus's children return to the custodial family, the folks back home are likely to complain, too. Their cry: the youngsters were overindulged.

"The children go to their father's house for a weekend of fun and gift-receiving," said Ed, the stepfather of three children who live with him, their mother, and their half sister, and visit their father and his girl friend every other weekend. "They come home Sunday night, bringing their laundry with them. They also bring their frustration at returning to real life. Their father is the good guy; their mother and I, the law enforcers."

It takes a while after each visit for children to adjust from being in one home to resettling in another, from relating to one family to living according to the rules of the other. Said a mother whose only son visits her ex-husband and his woman friend, "When my son walks in the door, I know at once if he's had a good time. If he has, he's close-mouthed. He's afraid *any* positive comment about what's going on in his father's home, in particular about the person I have come to refer to as 'that woman,' will upset me. If it's been a bad weekend, the complaints pour out.

"I know I'm to blame for my son's discomfort," she continued, "and I am trying to change. I have to convince my son that it's all right to talk about his father's friend. It's all right for him to like her and to tell me so, and I won't fall apart." She laughs. "But if he tells me one more time how *clean* it is at their place, I think I'll scream!"

It isn't easy to be a child with two families, to learn to feel at ease in a home that is not your own, then to have to reintegrate yourself into the custodial household. When both parents have formed new romantic relationships, the child must also reconcile his feelings about Father's new partner, Mother's new companion.

Ed commented on the change that takes place when his stepchildren return from visiting their father. "Inevitably, at least one of them will pick some sort of fight with me," he said. "It's their way of making sure I understand that I am not their father. I try to stay out of their way at those times, to give them space, to let them reconcile their feelings about different people and places."

Children aren't the only ones in restructured families who are anxious about homecoming. The parent and stepparent who remain at home must deal with fears of their own. What was it like in the host household, they wonder. Were the children welcomed by the stepparent? Were they made to feel at home? Did they feel *too much* at home? Comparisons between the two domiciles are inevitable. Which set of parents emerged more favorably?

Where the life styles in the two homes are markedly different (often the case), additional adjustments are called for.

Let us return to the sunny breakfast room of the modest one-family frame house that is home to Gloria, Arthur, and Matthew.

We had been concentrating on those times when Arthur's son Eric drops in on the family. Now let us consider Matthew's visits to *his* father, every other weekend and during some vacations. Waiting for Matthew at the other end of the train ride are his father, his stepmother, his stepsister, and his half sister. He is met and driven to a spacious and affluent home.

"When he returns," said Gloria, "those visits reverberate in *our* home. Matthew wants to know why *we* don't have a pinball machine, a microwave oven, and a magic-eye door that opens the way to the garage. Matthew wants to know why we don't have a boat. It doesn't take a genius to understand Matthew's discontent and I'll admit it makes me angry. I feel Matthew's values are all wrong, that he doesn't sufficiently appreciate the good life we've worked hard to create for him here. We can't compete with his father on economic terms, but there is so much of value that we do give him. I don't think Matthew recognizes that."

"Gloria is far more sensitive to the difference between the two homes than I," said Arthur. "I'm not competing with Matthew's father. We both have a lot to give the boy. Matthew's dad gives him boating and sports. I contribute music. From his father he gets exposure to new places and people. They do a lot of traveling abroad. From me, an interest in politics. More doors have been opened to Matthew (although not all by a magic eye) and I can't think that's bad for him."

The Case for Flexibility

Visitation schedules deserve to be respected. Appointments with one's children should be rescheduled only for very just cause. Children have to feel they can rely on a parent even (one might say *especially*) when they no longer live with one another. Breaking a date is a more serious matter when a home has been broken than when the family remains intact.

Children, on the other hand, should be granted greater flexibility in adhering to schedules. Special events in their lives must be considered. Perhaps a best friend is having a birthday party. Ask yourself: must your child turn down the invitation to attend because he or she is due at your home for the weekend? And keep in mind that the child who is resentful about having to visit is not likely to be a gracious guest. Dr. Richard Gardner strongly believes that a child's visitation schedule must not be rigid, but adds that the child must at the same time respect his parent's desire to spend time with him as well as the stepfamily's right to plan its own time. The child must understand that he is expected to tell the parent who does not have custody about any change of plans in advance.

Youngsters whose custodial arrangements mandate their being away from their home town every other weekend (when they visit their noncustodial parent) often find themselves precluded from involvement in Saturday clubs, sports teams, and the like. Not only do they leave their own friends behind in familiar territory, they usually do not find comfortable peer groups at the other end of the commute. This situation often results in the youngsters spending much concentrated time with their parent and stepparent. Not surprisingly, this seldom works out for the best. A good idea is to encourage the children (especially one who is an only child) to invite friends along on some visiting days. This relieves the pressure of too much togetherness and can add to the pleasure of a visit.

Nor should the distant parent and his spouse be overly sensitive if their adolescent children are less than overjoyed by the prospect of paying a visit to the welcoming homestead. Adolescence is a time of pulling away from family, of reaching toward independence. The teen-ager would rather be with friends than with anyone else. If the young person lived in an intact, nuclear family, he or she would be unlikely to want to spend much time with parents. Why, then, expect greater constancy in a remarried family? Again, flexibility and a sense of proportion are needed.

SOME OF THE CHILDREN SOME OF THE TIME

Where it is workable, it is wise to allow for variations in the guest roster. When several children visit, it is preferable to see some of the children some of the time and all of the children some of the time than it is to see all of the children all of the time. It is not always possible to stagger visits, however. Custody frequently is a weapon used by warring coparents, and relaxation of the rules may be waving a white flag. But persevere.

"In keeping with my divorce agreement, I was visited by all four of my children, together, every other weekend," said Burt.

"They stepped all over one another vying for my attention, and I knocked myself out trying to give it to them—in equal measure. By the end of each visit, I was exhausted and let down. I credit Ada, my present wife, with suggesting some reasonable plan in the midst of the chaos. 'Why don't you spend some time alone with one of the children, or take two out—not four—as you feel like it or as you perceive their need?' she suggested.

"My ex-wife was inflexible," Burt continued. "She wanted some time to have just to herself, she insisted, and I can't say that I blame her. So four children continued to arrive, every other weekend as before—but with a twist. Ada would plan an activity and go off with some of the children, leaving me to deal with the one I felt most needed my attention at the time. My oldest daughter was having problems in school. She and I went out for brunch one Sunday—just the two of us—and we had a long talk. I was able to help her see some of the issues more clearly.

"The following week, I phoned the guidance counselor at my daughter's school and could speak with him knowledgeably about my own child. That may not seem a major accomplishment, but I can tell you it is. The parent who gives up custody often is excluded from consultation with teachers, doctors, the very people who are guiding the children's lives. I even had to hire a lawyer to guarantee that I'd see my children's report cards. At first, the school refused to share such information with me."

Burt's is not an isolated case. Noncustodial parents have a right to information on how their children are doing in school. To their dismay, many have found they must fight to have this right recognized.

"Dealing with my daughter's problem made me feel less impotent as a father," Burt went on. "It underscored for my daughter the fact that, even though we no longer lived together, I still cared about her. The next weekend, I took the two younger children to a movie, and Ada and the two older ones spent some quiet hours around the house."

The children rebelled. The ones who did not get to be with their father complained about it. After each had enjoyed a special time, however, the benefits of the new arrangement became clear.

And what about Ada, the stepmother? "By dividing the group, I came to know Burt's children as individuals. Four was such an awesome number to relate to. I find I like some of them better than I do others. I find some of them are more responsive to me. One thing's for certain: I score much higher on a poll of the kids as individuals than I would have done if I'd been rated by group consensus."

7

Talking About Money

This chapter is titled "Talking About Money." In the remarried family, it often seems that's what everyone is doing: not just talking, but complaining, wheedling, cajoling, resenting—and using money for manipulating, punishing, rewarding, and maintaining ties that were severed by law.

"Money is the greatest impediment there is to a decent, well-mannered relationship between ex-partners," declares Patricia Lowe in her book, *The Cruel Stepmother.*

> It can, and usually does, embitter in one way or another both he who gives, whether willingly or by force or law, and she who takes, whether she feels it sufficient or is bitter because she must skimp to get by. And not only does it so affect the two principals, but their current spouses, if such exist. Unless all concerned have plenty of money, it may and probably will influence the climate between divorced parents and their offspring throughout the growing-up period. It touches decisions about education, housing, clothing, vacations, the medical and dental services chosen, and a whole raft of other problems sticky enough in their own right.

A counselor who works with stepfamilies is succinct. "The whole issue of money is a nightmare!" she declares.

A recurrent nightmare.

"Norbert pays 60 per cent of his income for alimony and child support," say Beverly, Norbert's second wife. "He really breaks his back to meet those payments and it makes me very angry. I have to work to help pay the household expenses, while his former wife hasn't worked a day in her life. She's thirty-six and healthier than I am.

"Their little girl hasn't shown up in a new dress *once* during the three years Norbert and I have been married." Beverly went on with her recital. "She arrives looking like a ragamuffin and—I can't help it—I become so angry. I know how much we send, and it's clear *that woman* can't be using the money for the children. I often find myself taking my anger out on the child simply because she's there, even though I know it hurts her to hear her mother criticized. But I'm only human. I'm not a saint.

"Norbert's ex-wife is constantly sending him letters demanding more money," Beverly complains. "When he receives one of those little love notes, which come about once a month, his mood changes dramatically. It's like he's having a period. He becomes difficult to live with. And I? Well, he tells me, I knew he had previous obligations when I agreed to marry him. So what right have *I* to complain!"

Talking about money is sometimes talking about other issues as well. Beverly resents the continued contact between her husband and his ex-wife—a contact that is maintained by the monthly letters that arrive as unwelcome guests in the remarried household, and that often have less to do with their stated subject—money—than they do with keeping the atmosphere in the new family emotionally charged.

When Norbert's daughter arrives, the pleasure of her visit is marred by the message she clearly delivers even before she's had time to take off her (threadbare) jacket and say hello. The carefully calculated disarray announces in banner headlines that Norbert has been remiss in living up to his obligations. (*See the awful state in which he has left his former family.*)

Father reacts to the provocation: "Gee, you look like a mess. With all the money I send your mother, she should be able to buy you better clothes. I can't take you out to dinner when you look like that." (*I am very generous. Your mother is misusing the money I send her.*)

This use of the children as message bearers to express the malevolent wishes of one parent to the other is not uncommon in sequential families. It is neither subtle nor sound.

A stepmother responded to misrepresentation, by her predecessor, of how much was being contributed by her husband for his children's upkeep by frequently raising the subject of money to her stepsons. In no uncertain manner, she let them know their father was indeed supporting them, and at no insignificant sacrifice to himself or to his current family. During one visit, as the stepmother enumerated the expenses for everything from orthodontics to tennis sneakers, her younger stepson exploded, "For God's sake, lay off. I'm sick and tired of hearing about money all the time!"

He knew she was talking about more than money.

While money can be a false issue that serves to keep alive many of the conflicts between two people who were formerly married to one another, it often is a real issue as well. In most remarried families, there simply isn't enough to go around—not enough time, not enough love, not enough money. This reality cannot be glossed over. In the stepfamily, the subject of money and everyone's feelings about it has to be raised and talked about or resentments will fester.

The time for a couple to begin to talk about money—how much (or how little) there is and their attitudes toward it—is before they enter a second marriage. When either partner has obligations from a previous marriage, the situation must be clearly laid out. Certain conditions, such as alimony and child support payments, can place a tremendous economic burden on a marriage. The ongoing need to meet monthly payments often causes resentment not only in the stepparent but in the parent as well. But the obligation exists, and the remarrying family must face up to it as a fact of their life.

"We do live in a society where we've been socialized to think that men take care of women," says Nina Cohen, a psychologist who is also a second wife and stepmother. "When your husband is supporting his former wife and a prior family, he can't fully support his second wife. This may affect the remarried couple's decision to have a mutual child."

When the honeymoon's over, the second wife who finds herself in this situation may have second thoughts. She may grow to resent her husband for denying parenthood to her. She may also resent her stepchildren; but for them, she could have had children of her own. "Every woman wants to be a princess," says Dr. Cohen. "It doesn't make sense, but it's real.

"The man has the mirror image of that fantasy," she continues. "He believes he should be able to support his new wife and any family they might have. And when he can't (as many men cannot), it tears him apart."

A woman who considers marriage to a man who is a father should know the financial obligations of her prospective spouse. Like the stereotypical father of the bride, it is she who must demand some solid answers to some very unromantic questions, to better understand the prospects for her future. What income is there? How is it to be spent? On alimony? Child support? Do prior mortgages have to be paid off? How is the children's education to be underwritten? Will there be enough money for college?

When her husband found himself suddenly out of work, one stepmother saw most of her salary going to support her young stepchildren at a very expensive prep school. When she suggested the children be withdrawn from the prestigious institution they attended and registered at schools in their community, her husband behaved as if this "wicked stepmother" had advised taking the bread from his children's mouths. "That's completely out of the question," he exploded. "The young people in my family have always attended ————!"

Who will work in the new marriage? Is work optional for either partner? Obligatory for both? If the answer is yes, the new wife must consider how she feels about that. Is she willing to sacrifice having her own family, if that must be the decision she and her husband come to? Will she then feel free to accept her husband's children?

The man who weds a woman and becomes stepfather to her children should ask about arrangements for the youngster's support—which expenses will be covered by their father, which ones he may be expected to assume. He would do well to realize that some power always comes with money. If the former husband is footing the bills, more than likely the stepfather will have to accept a supporting role in the lives of his stepchildren, even if he lives with them and interacts with them daily. Their father will play the lead.

One divorced man who became a noncustodial father and then married again, setting up house with his new wife and her children, describes the change in his role as he moved from one household to the other: "I went from being breadwinner to cookie supplier."

Where the children's father *fails* to come through with the bread, the would-be stepfather must face his feelings about assuming financial responsibility for another man's children.

"Calvin seems to be forever behind in sending the piddling amount he's required to pay toward the support of his son, Jesse," says Jesse's stepfather, Robert, a young stockbroker who is just beginning to grow accustomed to professional success. "My wife has asked Calvin to pay half the tuition to the private school their son attends. Calvin's answer was that we ought to be living in the suburbs and sending Jesse to the local grade school. How do you like that? He refuses to pay *anything* toward Jesse's education, then calls and asks to be more involved—to go to meetings, confer with teachers, and so on. We told him, 'If you pay, you participate.'

"It's not that Calvin can't afford it," Robert went on. "He's unattached, lives in a nice apartment, drives a good car, and has a regular appointment with a shrink. The trouble is, he knows that when the shouting's over I'm going to come through for his son. And I do. Then *he* buys the boy a Mickey Mouse watch and, to judge by Jesse's reaction, his is the greatest, most generous father in the whole wide world. It makes me furious. You know what I'd like to do with that watch!"

Another stepfather calculates he has spent $50,000 to support his stepchildren because their father refuses to pay. Yet his stepdaughter still says, "My father would have bought me that," whenever her stepfather turns down a request.

Of all the issues that the stepfamily must confront, none has the ability to make so many so *furious* as does money. When the ex-wife fails to receive the support payment on time, she becomes furious. Many also become vindictive and *punish* their former husbands by denying the fathers' rights to see their own children.

When the current wife sees her husband struggle to meet his commitment, and then be denied the right to see his youngsters if he defaults, *she* becomes furious. "My husband lost his job and was out of work for four months," said a second wife. "It was a terrible time for him and for us, one that was made even worse when his ex-wife refused him permission to see their children *until he was up to date in his payments.*"

Too often, families in conflict draw a correlation between support payments and access to the children. This hurts all who are involved—especially the children—and benefits only the lawyers, *when* they are called in and if *they* are successful in collecting their fees.

It is important to encourage visitation between children and the parent with whom they do not reside. Dr. Lee Salk cautions, "It's certainly never in the best interests of the child to be used as an instrument of barter."

A man and woman who are considering a match that will merge his children with hers should give some thought to merging their economic life styles. Will there be problems? Do one parent's children stand to derive special benefits from the nonresident parent—or the grandparents? Is there a Santa Claus Daddy in the picture? (More about *him* later.) If so, problems of financial inequity are sure to arise. The couple should talk this over (perhaps with a counselor *before* they make the arrangements legal) and come up with some plan about how such matters will be handled.

When finances in the blended family differ appreciably from those of any outside parent, an insistence on equality can sometimes be as damaging as is overindulgence. Libby Walker, who was associated with the Remarriage Consultation Service of the Jewish Board of Family and Children's Services, tells two stories.

In one, a father gave his son half the cost of a tennis racket and told the boy, "Your mother will contribute the other half." But the mother and her husband couldn't afford to pay the balance. In the second incident, the father contributed half the cost of a guitar for his daughter, knowing full well that the girl's mother and stepfather would have a very hard time matching his share.

"I keep picturing these two kids—one plucking half a guitar, the other swinging half a tennis racket!" said Libby Walker.

If a couple plans children of the current union, their financial burden will increase. They should give some thought to how this will affect the family, and budget accordingly. The stepsiblings can almost be counted on to voice some objections to any change in status. Said one struggling young actor, "My wife's daughters griped about our having to cut down on our weekend activities after our baby was born. We now have additional expenses and can no longer take the children out to dinner and a movie every weekend. We can't plan a vacation this coming summer. Their mother and I told the girls we were sorry they were disappointed, but the decision to have the baby was ours. We hoped, in time, they'd come to think it had all been worthwhile."

Family counselors go so far as to suggest that *before* the wedding is not too soon for a remarrying couple to consider how their money will be handled in their wills.

While all this may sound unromantic, a contrasting unrealistic approach to remarriage—one that relies on the belief that love will conquer all—often results in an all-too-realistic redivorce.

"Economic polygamy requires a mature sense of economic responsibility on everyone's part," declares writer Davidyne Mayleas in her book, *Rewedded Bliss*. She continues: "Unreal financial demands by an ex-wife can severely cripple the functioning of a new family and, by so doing, reduce the monies available for everyone. Unwarranted miserliness by remarriers can only damage the children of the previous marriage. Adults who share the parenthood of children have to learn to talk to each other, to make treaties. . . ."

Mayleas proposes a plan to gain this rapport. She suggests the husband and his new wife invite the ex-spouse to sit in on a family budget session and cooperate in examining expenses so that everyone has a good idea of what money is realistically available for the support of the families involved.

This, of course, presupposes good will, an absence of rancor— in short, a more perfect world than that in which an overwhelming number of stepfamilies find themselves.

How, then, are they coping—these nontraditional families who join together in love and good will, albeit fettered by previous and future obligations? Many are arriving at some nontraditional arrangements, some of which work out very well indeed.

"We have not got into a lot of money problems," said Tom, a father whose five children live with his former wife and who now makes his home with Stacy, his present wife, and her three children. Eight children in all. How can there *not* be money problems?

"It's really very simple," Tom explained. "Stacy supports her children and I take care of mine. We had to deal with that before we married.

"We have an interesting setup," he went on. "In the property settlement, I left the house and everything to my first wife. I didn't want my children to have to move. Stacy owns the home we now live in. She's always owned her own home; she sold the old one to buy this one, so we could move into a place that was new for our marriage. She's a very strong woman; her first husband, an alcoholic, has not contributed a cent toward the children's expenses. Stacy has managed everything by herself.

"She continues to support the basic household, pays for gas, electricity, phone, groceries. I pay my equitable portion of room and board. When my children come to stay for a while, I know the expenses will go up, and I pick up the grocery bills so they will not be a burden.

"It's an unorthodox arrangement," Tom admits, "but then every man doesn't have to support five children from a previous marriage!"

TWO-INCOME HOUSEHOLDS

Not all remarried women are as financially independent as Stacy. Nevertheless, the working wife is no longer a rarity. Recent figures show about 52.8 per cent of all American wives are employed or actively looking for jobs, a jump of ten percentage points in the last decade. If the study were to differentiate between first-wed wives and those who've been married more than once, I daresay the percentage of working women would be higher in the latter category. Following the dissolution of a marriage (either by divorce or the death of a mate), many women re-enter the work force out of economic necessity or in an attempt to reconstruct their lives. In the renewal process, the working woman becomes more independent. She knows the feeling, often for the first time, of having her own money, and she likes it. When she plights her troth the second time around, she does not pledge her pocketbook.

Penny had her Ph.D. in economics well in hand when she met and married Edgar, who had been divorced from his first wife and was responsible for the support of his three young children. Before her marriage, Penny had lived well as a single woman. She traveled far and frequently, dressed fashionably and expensively, and was able to indulge most of her whims. Marriage changed that free-and-easy life style.

Edgar often was hard pressed to pay his bills. He was burdened by his financial commitments. Penny and Edgar live very modestly. Here's how they divide their economic responsibilities. They each have separate accounts and share a joint account. Penny pays for her expenses—clothing, business costs, tennis lessons ("an indulgence," she admits)—out of her account. Edgar takes care of his needs *and* pays for child support out of his account. *After* he has subtracted the money he sends to his children, he and Penny contribute equal amounts to a joint account, out of which they struggle to cover their joint obligations and extravagances (rent, groceries, vacations, entertainment).

"It would kill me to see *my* money going to support Edgar's children," says Penny. And so it does not.

Hannah is an editor, Phillip a curator at a historical museum. Both have children from previous marriages who do not live with them. In Hannah's first-go-round, she was the wife of a prosperous businessman. Money was not a problem. Today, she has complete responsibility for her own support. Phillip sends money for

his three children, the oldest of whom is in college, plus alimony
to their mother. Hannah and Phillip each pays half the cost of
running their home. "When my children come to stay with us,"
said Hannah, "I pick up three-quarters of our household expenses. Phillip does the same when his children are with us. It's
all perfectly fair.

"And a little bit cold," she added. Lower mobility is not easy to
take.

It's much less of an adjustment to remarry richer.

When Helen married Jim, a film producer, she moved into a
more affluent world than she'd known with her first husband, who
was a teacher. Between husbands, Helen returned to school,
earned a master's degree in business administration, and landed a
job in the business office of a television network. There she met
Jim. The couple share a sprawling ranch home with Helen's two
daughters and, often, Jim's two sons. Proud of her new role as a
wage earner, Helen insists on covering the girl's expenses (although it is not necessary), pays for schools, camps, allowances.

Jim supports his sons, pays all expenses of the combined household, and covers "group costs." "We eat out frequently, go to the
theater often, and vacation lavishly," he explained. "We spend
more freely than the children's other parents. While I realize that
may put them at a disadvantage, I like to live in style, and I can
afford it."

Helen's former husband is defensive, and hence comes across as
critical. "Your stepfather likes things rather splashy," he tells his
daughters. "That's why he's sunk all that money into that show
place of a house, why he feels a need to run off to Europe whenever the spirit moves him." The girls are torn between feelings of
loyalty to their father and feelings of guilt. The fact is, they enjoy
living in the show place and accompanying their mother and stepfather on European jaunts.

This should not come as a surprise to their father. If he did not
see himself in competition with his children's other family, he
could more easily express interest (and perhaps some pleasure) in
the new experiences now possible for his children. If the girls saw
that their father was genuinely pleased for them, they'd be much
more relaxed during their visits with him. They could share their

new life, not hide it. They could try for the best of two possible worlds.

The Santa Claus Syndrome

The opposite situation, and the one that crops up as a problem very often in remarried families, is when children spend their everyday lives with their mother and stepfather, go off for good-time weekends with their father who has ceased to be the head of the house, the disciplinarian, and has become instead the gift giver, the Santa Claus Daddy. On the West Coast, he's called the Disneyland Daddy. By any name, he is described by the custodial family as the parent who does not have a daily relationship with his children, one in which parent is both praiser and punisher, but is instead the weekend wonder worker. There need be no correlation between his generosity and his ability to indulge his children. The Santa Claus Daddy pays out of guilt.

Janey has been badgering her mother and stepfather for new skis, boots, and bindings. The couple considers such an expenditure an extravagance. Janey goes skiing no more than three times each winter, they point out. At eleven, she is still growing. She can rent ski equipment whenever it's necessary, they say. Janey spends Christmas vacation with her dad. Presto! New skis.

"Suddenly, money substitutes for affection," believes Jeannette Lofas, coauthor of *Living in Step*. "The children get merchandise from the nonresident parent. The message he imparts is: See *how much* I love you."

A stepfather is talking about his stepchildren's father: "We're constantly asking him not to be a sugar daddy."

Father responds: "I have to make up to my daughter for not seeing her."

The guilty father satisfies no one. When he is generous to a fault, he frustrates any efforts of the custodial family to give the children a sense of what is financially appropriate. The children learn that no decree is final, for papa will pay. With parents living in two separate homes, many children learn quickly how to manipulate one family against the other.

Father's new wife also resents her husband's indulgence of his children, in some situations because she stands aside and sees her husband being manipulated, and it hurts. In other cases, the complaints of the stepmother are based on less altruistic reasons. For the second wife, money often is the medium for a test of power: *Who do you love more—me or the children? Will you buy them toys or buy me trifles?*

One stepmother stated with candor (made possible by two years in marital therapy): "I used to resent it every time my husband took a walk with his daughter and came back with a gift he'd bought for the little girl. I gave as my reason the fact that he contributed enough of his hard-earned money for her support, and this was an additional and unnecessary expense. In reality, I was jealous of an eight-year-old. I wanted my husband to bring some flowers for me, not to spend his time and his thoughts on picking up something that might bring pleasure to his daughter.

"I think I now have a much healthier attitude toward my husband's relationship with my stepdaughter," the young woman added. "I understand his need to be giving, to be spontaneous. At times, however, I continue to be distressed by his sugar-daddy splurges. I don't think it's good for the little girl. I'm not asking him to deny his daughter Santa Claus, but I do try to remind him that the kind old man arrives with his bounty but one night of the three hundred and sixty-five that make up the year."

8

And Then There's Ours

"Shall we have a child of our own?"

Unless age and physical condition clearly preclude the remarried couple from producing a child of the marriage, this question, more than likely, crosses their minds.

Reponses vary according to a number of considerations:

● Whether one or both partners have children from previous marriages (where only one is a parent, the couple is more likely to have a child than when both husband and wife enter the marriage with children).

● The attitudes of husband and wife toward parenthood (the traditional assumption that every woman wants to become a mother is erroneous. Of the couples I interviewed, about half who had a child of the current marriage did so at the urging of the husband).

● The ages of husband and wife.

● The ages and sexes of children already present.

● How secure participants feel about the current marriage (in second or third marriages as in first-time-arounds, having a baby may be an affirmation of the soundness of the relationship or it may be viewed as an attempt to save a faltering marriage).

● Existing financial obligations.

CAN THE MARRIAGE AFFORD ANOTHER CHILD?

For many remarrieds whose budgets already have been stretched to support children of former marriages and, often, for-

mer spouses as well, two incomes may be a precondition of the
merger and having "our baby" an impossibility.

Such was the situation that Greta, a capable young real estate
saleswoman, found herself in when she married Steve. She was
then twenty-eight. It was her first marriage, his second. Steve was
responsible for the support of three young children born to him
and his first wife, to whom he also paid alimony. Steve is a police-
man.

Greta knew she and Steve wouldn't be able to have children. "It
takes both our salaries to pay our rent, take care of our own
needs, *and* meet Steve's obligations," she said. "That much was
clear to me before I agreed to marry Steve. Still, it was a very
hard decision for me to make, never to have children of my own.
It proved not to be insurmountable, but it was (and still is) painful for me to accept."

Even when finances permit, the parent-partner may feel that existent children demand enough of an emotional investment from
him. He does not look to the remarriage for parenthood; indeed,
additional children who would call for additional involvement
would be unwelcome. It is important for someone going into a
marriage with these terms to know and accept the ground rules.

In previous chapters, we've noted that many a man and woman
saunters into the stepfamily without any idea of the realities of living with other people's children—and difficulties ensue. Let us
note here that there are also those individuals who marry without
any idea of what it will be like to act as a stepparent to someone
else's children and *not* to have children of one's own.

Some find this an ideal situation. "I always knew I'd be a perfect stepmother," said a successful editor, who entered her first
(and only) marriage when she was thirty-seven. "I absolutely
wanted to marry a man who had children. I like young people,
but I don't feel a need to mother them. I enjoy those weekends
and vacations when my husband's children come for a visit, and
I'm also pleased when they leave. We're able to go on with our
lives and our careers."

Still others have regrets similar to those expressed by writer
Jean Baer in her book, *The Second Wife:* "I regret that I listened

to my husband and gave up the chance to have a child who would be ours. For often I think men who remarry say one thing that stems from their past—and may subsequently feel a different way."

Suppose, then, that husband and wife decide in favor of becoming parents. Are they being selfish? Is this a fair thing to do to children who existed before this marriage took place, to children who have experienced so many changes in their lives?

It is hard to predict what the effect of having "our child" will be on the couple and on any "his" or "her" children who exist. In general, family experts are optimistic.

To the query, "Will it add to the tensions of our blended family if my husband and I have a child of our own?" Dr. Fitzhugh Dodson replies:

My answer is yes—and no. In some stepfamilies, the new baby becomes a psychological link between the two families. But in others it can be a negative factor. For example, if the family includes only one spouse's children, who do not get along well with the stepparent, the new infant may be looked upon as one more wedge coming between them and their natural parent. And so the [new] child may be greatly resented. There are many variables that affect this situation: the ages and sexes of the children, the temperaments of both children and adults, the relationship between stepparent and stepchildren before the birth of the baby, and more.

Don't decide whether or not to have a child by its possible effect on the stepchildren. Decide it the way you would if you were a husband and wife with no stepchildren to consider. That is, if having a child is important to you and your marriage, then have it. If not, don't.

Marriage, family, and child counselor Thelma Kaplan offers a somewhat different view. "You should not have the new child while you're still working out your own relationships and those with the present children," she advises.

She presents an example of a family that came to her for counseling. "He had two children, she had two children. All four youngsters were close in age (between eight and twelve years old) and he wanted a joint child."

There were, it comes as no surprise, issues to be resolved in the combined family. All of its members were seen in therapy, sometimes separately and at times together. The children's problems were attributable to just plain jealousy: of one another and of their parents' affection for each other and for the different children. But the parents' difficulties were more complex.

The counselor explained: "The father, who'd been sole parent to his two children for several years, was so relieved to have someone take over as head of the family, he abdicated his parental role entirely. He became a bystander, leaving all decision-making to his wife. She, in turn, resented his putting so much weight on her. Instead of being the helpmeet she'd expected to find, he'd deposited two more children in her care—and now he wanted to saddle her with a fifth child!

"In addition," Thelma Kaplan went on, "neither adult had made peace with the absent parties—the ghosts of the past—and it is essential that you do that before you can deal with the present or plan for the future. After one year in therapy, this man and woman were ready to have a baby. And they did."

When a couple is ready to have a child, and if present children are struggling with no more than the "ordinary problems" of family rearrangement, the new child may, in fact, serve to bring *his* and *her* children together. "Our child" is the one thing in the marriage they have in common. Said the father in a combination family, "My children and my wife's children still have little to do with one another. Their temperaments just don't mesh. But they all care about the baby."

When "Our Baby" Is the First Child of One of the Parents, Some Special Considerations Emerge

Adjustment seems easier when both husband and wife have children from previous marriages. Where only one has been a parent, that partner often tends to sit in judgment of the actions and reactions of the other, much as is done in combined families. *Is she treating our child with more kindness (love, understanding) than she does mine?* the parent wonders. This kind of scrutiny makes the person who is the stepparent (and now also a natural parent) much less spontaneous about her own behavior—to whichever child or children.

In the words of one woman: "If I criticize Jason, who is our mutual child, we're comfortable with that. But if I criticize Glynis or Daniel (my husband's children), I'm more cautious and he hears it differently."

A young woman who wed a widower who was father to two young sons was elated when she learned she was going to have a baby. Her joy was short-lived. "When I told my husband I was pregnant," she recalled, "he immediately *warned* me not to get wrapped up in the baby and neglect his boys. That's how the happy event (it was a planned pregnancy, I should tell you) was welcomed in our home. Having a mutual child didn't draw us together as a family; it added a player to my team."

The birth of a common child leads each of the marriage partners to reassess his or her relationships with any and all existent children and both the natural parent's and stepparent's attitudes toward them.

When Barbara was pregnant with Caryn Sue, her first and only child, she worried about whether her husband Hal would love the coming baby as much as he did his daughter Linda. Said Barbara, "I feared having our baby would renew Hal's feelings of guilt for having abandoned Linda.

"The words may sound strong," she added, "but I know Hal believed that's what he had done when he moved out of the home and initiated divorce proceedings against his first wife, who is Linda's mother. I was afraid Hal's guilt would stand in the way of his making the kind of commitment I hoped for to our child."

"Barbara's fears weren't completely off the mark," Hal admitted, his glance falling on his winsome younger daughter, now almost two years old, who played nearby. "Of course I love Caryn Sue," he said, "but having her has renewed the pain I feel about being unable to have a natural relationship with Linda—not seeing her every day, not being there for her whenever she needs or wants me. It hurts me more every time Linda's visit with us draws to an end, and I see one of my daughters staying while the other prepares to go to *her* home. Barbara is better able to understand my pain now than she was before she became a mother. It's been a mellowing experience for Barbara. All things considered, having Caryn Sue has been good for us all."

Until she herself became a mother, Barbara had been a long-suffering stepmother. She regarded Linda as her rival for Hal's attention, and tried to squelch her resentment of the time father and daughter spent together. At the same time, she believed the public (her family and friends) viewed Linda as a reflection of her. (There it is again, the feeling that everyone is scrutinizing the stepparent, the vision of life as a stage on which one must deliver a perfect performance.) So Barbara chafed when Hal's daughter, Linda, didn't arrive with a suitcase filled with clothes that would have suited Barbara's taste. (But she wouldn't go out and buy anything for the child because Hal paid quite enough money for child support, thank you—what *was* that woman doing with all that money? Clearly not spending it on Linda . . .) She bristled at the untidyness of Linda's hair, and she felt herself annoyed when Linda fidgeted at the dinner table, and she cringed when Linda whined. . . . What would people think? How could she take Linda anywhere? Why didn't Hal take a more active role in Linda's upbringing?

"Then, when I was preparing to be a real mother myself," said Barbara, "I decided to stop my ersatz mothering of Linda and prepare for the real thing. That was a liberating decision I should have reached a long time before. It freed me from the pressure of trying to make Linda into a perfect child. It freed her from my constant nagging, and it freed Hal of the burden of mediation between two people he cared about and didn't want to see hurting one another. After I had Caryn Sue, I realized I'd been very hard on Linda."

Said Hal, "I think Barbara had to come face-to-face with real parenting to learn there are no perfect children. She found out children are going to get dirty, that they'll be noisy, that there are times when even a child you love very much—your own child—is going to get on your nerves."

Becoming a mother made Barbara a better stepmother.

ABOUT CHILDREN'S FEELINGS

Although in the long run having a baby seems to be good for the reconstituted family,* in the short run many of the children already in the family must come to grips with some troubling matters.

Seven-year-old Gregory greeted the news of his mother's pregnancy with apparent calm. The usual questions were asked: "When will the baby be born? Where will it sleep? What are you going to name it?"

Gregory received reassuring answers: "The baby will be born in May; it will sleep in the den, which will be redecorated as a nursery; Heather, if it's a girl. We're considering naming him Christopher if it's a boy."

Gregory lives with his mother and stepfather, Theo. He has a warm and close relationship with his natural father and he carries his father's surname. Two months before the birth of Christopher (it *was* a boy), Gregory exploded into tears. "But the baby's name will be different from mine," he sobbed. "The baby will have Theo's name. Nobody else will know the baby belongs to me."

What's in a name? When brothers and sisters carry different surnames, the answer may be: a lot.

In a stepfamily we visited earlier, Linda and Caryn Sue have the same surname, for they have the same father. Unlike Gregory, however, Linda does not live in the same home as her half-sibling. After Caryn Sue was born, those who interacted with Linda as she went about the routine of her daily life failed to recognize that

---

* Sociologist Lucile Duberman reported the results of her study of 88 reconstituted families in Ohio: "We found that of those families who had had children together, 78% rated excellent in their relationships between stepchildren and stepparents, compared to 53% of those who did not have children together. It can be inferred from this that the presence of natural children in a reconstituted family enhances the relationships between stepchildren and stepparents." Lucile Duberman, *The Reconstituted Family: A Study of Remarried Couples and Their Children* (Chicago: Nelson-Hall, 1975), p. 71.

life had changed considerably for the young girl, that Linda was a sister now.

An incident described by Hal is especially poignant. "After we had Caryn Sue, we phoned and told Linda the good news. She was the first person we called, even before we told Barbara's parents. Linda was thrilled," Hal said. "She really was, and she wanted to share her excitement. At the next meeting of her Brownie troop, she announced to one and all that she had a new sister. And what do you think that genius of a Girl Scout leader did? She told Linda, 'No you don't. The baby has a different mother than you do. She's only your half sister. That doesn't count.'

"When I heard about that incident, my blood boiled," said Hal, upset again at the very recollection of the encounter.

The following weekend, when Linda came to visit, Barbara and Hal saw her tiptoe into the baby's room and look down at the crib where Caryn Sue lay sleeping. "I don't care what *anyone* says," Linda whispered emphatically. "You are so my sister. I *know* you are."

As Caryn Sue grows older, she will have to work out *her* relationship with Linda and try to understand Linda's connection to her family. Right now, the little girl knows Linda is her sister. "[But] she doesn't really understand what a sister is," says Hal. "Soon, we'll have to explain to her why she lives with us and her sister does not, why both girls call me Daddy but Linda calls my wife Barbara. Because I remarried across religious lines, we'll also have to explain why Linda goes to synagogue with her mother and Caryn Sue attends church with *her* mother. There are going to be lots of questions, that much is certain. I'm not so certain we'll be able to come up with satisfactory answers."

Hal and Barbara, as participants in nontraditional families, are struggling to find solutions to some very nontraditional challenges —in this case, the workable merger of family past with family present. Some of today's stepfamilies see themselves as taking on the challenge of building what *may* be the family of the future.

Bill Davis, Shellie Ames, Shellie's two daughters, Gabriella, fifteen, and Nicole, twelve, and Bill and Shellie's son, Gideon, age one, constitute one such family. Thirty-four-year-old Bill, a settlement worker, is deeply committed to the Mexican-American community he serves. Shellie, thirty-five, is a dancer-choreographer who is busily involved in California's theatrical community. Her daughters move between Shellie's world and the affluent life of their father Gil, a Nevada rancher.

Shortly after Bill met Shellie, he moved out of his simple bachelor apartment and into the large house (complete with backyard pool and orange trees) that became Shellie's as part of the settlement of her divorce from Gil. ("I felt like a boarder," Bill admits, "not only because Shellie and I weren't married, but because there I was in a house I never could have afforded.") Bill and Shellie decided to get married.

"I did not, and do not now, see myself as any kind of surrogate father to Shellie's daughters," Bill said. "I came into these young women's lives when they were just that—precocious, bright, developed, liberated young women. They have a warm, loving relationship with their mother, and their father is very important to them *as* a father and as a male figure.

"I have a good deal of affection for the girls," he explained, "but I have some difficulty in telling them how I feel about them —probably because they aren't my daughters. Gabriella, the older of Shellie's daughters, and I get along very well. That's probably because she accepted me immediately as a person. Nicole is very suspicious of me, and very troubled. She's still fighting her parents' divorce, even though both her mother and father have remarried, and she's also fighting me.

"Having a stepparent can be quite beneficial for adolescent youngsters," Bill noted, speaking both as a stepfather and as a social worker. "It provides them with a parentlike figure against whom society says it is really quite acceptable to rebel."

When Shellie and Bill decided to have a mutual child (largely because Bill wanted to become a parent; Shellie was not so certain she wanted to be involved in baby care again), they sold Shellie's home and moved to a much more modest place (no pool) along the coast, closer to the settlement house where Bill works. They decided their baby would be born there.

Soon, Shellie became pregnant. Bill and Shellie broke the news to the girls, who reacted as their parents had anticipated. Gabriella was ecstatic. Nicole saw herself displaced as younger child in the family.

"We made it clear that this was something Bill and I had decided," Shellie said. "We were not asking my daughters' permission. Rather, we'd come to an adult decision, which we shared with them. We also planned to have the baby at home. If the girls wished to fully share the experience with us, however, we did impose one condition."

That condition was that the girls attend natural childbirth classes with their mother and stepfather, so they'd know what to expect when the baby was born. Gabriella became a regular member of the class. Nicole attended less often than more, but she too was present one somewhat crisp December morning, along with the midwife and friends and relatives of Shellie and Bill, to witness the birth and to welcome Gideon Ames-Davis to the world.

Gil, Shellie's first husband, was among the welcomers.

"You're probably wondering about that," said Shellie, "and I don't blame you. Gabriella and Nicole came to Bill and me to request that Gil be invited. Not just invited . . . they wanted him to be named godfather to the baby. 'Otherwise,' they said, 'he'll be the only one in our family who has no tie to our brother.'

"You can see the extent of their definition of family," said Shellie. "I relented on inviting their father, but I drew the line at including his new wife and her children, too."

Gideon came into the world on a Saturday morning. Saturday afternoon found his half sisters and *their* father at Disneyland. What better location for a celebration!

Declared Bill Davis, father of Gideon, stepfather of Gabriella and Nicole, "Don't you think we'll have to come up with new rites and rituals to meet the needs of the kinds of sequential families being established today?"

Is Gideon Ames-Davis the future of the family?

9

Reconstructing the Family
After a Parent Has Died

Sounds of a steel band echoed down to the white beach where, recumbent on canvas chaise longues, Sharon and Ted sipped banana daiquiris and squinted at the waves lapping up on the sand. The sun was warming, the sky cloudless. Following a whirlwind seven-week courtship, the tranquillity of their Caribbean honeymoon was welcome.

The idyl was interrupted, Sharon recalls, by the arrival of one of the hotel bellhops. A message for Ted. A phone call to be returned.

Sharon remembers thinking the call was from the couple she and Ted had met in the nightclub the previous evening, the first following their arrival. They'd had a few drinks together. It had been pleasant. There had been talk of getting together for tennis. . . .

It was, instead, Ted's mother, calling from New England. Ted's son, Alex, had set fire to the master bedroom in his home. The honeymoon, all too literally, was over. Ted and Sharon flew back to the States.

When she first met Ted, over dinner at the home of mutual friends, Sharon learned he was a widower with two small children. She voiced appropriate regrets and went on to other topics. She gave the matter little thought. She found she was very attracted to Ted, to his dark good looks, his self-assurance, his worldliness. Sharon was quiet where Ted was outgoing, unself-consciously pretty but thought herself plain, a country girl enjoying her first teaching job in a medium-sized city. Ted was a partner in a successful law firm.

On their first date, two nights later, Sharon learned Ted's wife, Norma, had died in childbirth. The baby, Hope, was delivered in good health. She was now two years old; her older brother, Alex, was five and a half. A housekeeper cared for the two children. Ted took a photograph from his wallet. Two beautiful, dark-eyed young children smiled at the camera.

Sharon asked few questions about the youngsters. Later, they figured little in her decision to marry Ted. After all, she reasoned, she handled a classroom of twenty-two children every day; surely there'd be no problem just caring for two! "I think," says Sharon, looking backward, "there was something in me that looked forward to having an instant family. I was a nice person. Why *shouldn't* Ted's children love me and I them?"

Sharon's expectations were unrealistic; they also were typical of the instant parent: I love you; I will love your children. She was angry and disappointed with herself when she admitted she did not love the children; she felt like a failure when she realized the two orphaned youngsters presented much more of a challenge than the twenty-two children she had managed every day.

What had not been apparent in the photograph was how deeply disturbed Ted's older child was, how much anger he felt at the death of his mother, and how much help he would need in learning, first, to express that anger and to do so appropriately. Studies have shown that the loss of a parent before age six is devastating to a child, yet Alex had never been allowed to go through the mourning process at all. When Norma died, friends and relatives of the family rallied round to protect the young boy. The decision was made that Alex should not attend his mother's funeral, that he should be spared the trauma. This encouraged him to build up a fantasy that his mother had not died, that she'd only deserted the family and someday would return.

A family friend came and took Alex to live with her while the family came to grips with the tragedy. Two weeks later, he was returned to his own home to find his mother still absent. What's more, the nurturing parent had been replaced by a rival: a baby sister who demanded and received attention from everyone. For a long time, it seemed to Alex, the house was filled with people. His grandparents came and went, his aunts and uncles, distant relatives, family friends. His father sometimes talked to the people, but a lot of the time he just stayed in his room. "Don't disturb your daddy," Alex was admonished. "He's tired and needs to rest."

Ted mourned privately, offering Alex no opportunity to join him in mutual grieving. Thus the boy was able to continue to build a fantasy that his mother really did not die. This is not an unusual reaction for the young child. "It's almost as if they deny the parent is dead," explains psychiatrist Lee Salk. "They feel he or she is only away on a trip, and is expected back someday. The marriage of the remaining parent is the equivalent of saying that the absent parent is really dead. This sometimes brings on a grief reaction that may not have been expressed at the time of death. And even if it were felt before, you may find a transitory hostility and aggressiveness on the part of the child toward the new parent because it seems as if he or she is replacing the dead parent."

When his father took a new wife, Alex finally was forced to confront the reality of his mother's death. Although two full years had gone by since that tragic event, the upcoming marriage marked the onset of belated mourning for the boy. Offers of sympathy would have been appropriate; instead, Alex was offered congratulations. "Isn't it wonderful, you'll be getting a new mother," he was told by his housekeeper, his relatives, the parents of his friends, all of whom were pleased to see the family reconstitute itself. Wonderful? When his father and stepmother were on their honeymoon, Alex showed everyone how wonderful he thought it was. He set fire to their bed.

It was the first of a series of fires, the beginning of years of anguish. "If it hadn't been for the children, I doubt Ted and I would have remained together," said Sharon. "Of course, if it hadn't been for the children, we wouldn't have faced so many problems," she added wryly.

Sharon blamed herself for Alex's hostility. *It was all her fault. She was not a good mother. Norma would have known how to handle the boy.* It didn't help matters that Ted shared, even encouraged, that harsh evaluation. THE GREATEST THREAT TO THE SUCCESS OF A REMARRIAGE THAT FOLLOWS UPON THE DEATH OF A

SPOUSE IS THE TENDENCY OF THE SURVIVORS TO IDEALIZE THE
DEAD PARTNER.

Ted recalled Norma as the perfect wife and mother: understanding, good-humored, intelligent, loving, someone devoted to
the care and nurture of her family—to sum it up, a beautiful
saint. This was the legacy of their mother that he handed down to
his children. Faced with this competition, how could any stepparent hope to measure up?

"Whenever I had unkind thoughts about Alex—and believe me,
he gave me reason to think unkindly," said Sharon, "Ted accused
me of being the wicked stepmother. I began to believe he must be
right. I had so little faith in myself. After all, I'd never been a parent before. Ted was the one with all the experience, and he was
clear enough about telling me I was doing a terrible job.

"Once, following one of our many fights in which he raged on
and on, listing my shortcomings, and I cowered and cried, feeling myself a failure, Ted went out and bought me a book called
The Cruel Stepmother. He insisted I read it to find out what I
was. . . . When I suggested we send Alex to camp the summer
the boy was ten, for the boy's sake and to give us a much-needed
breather, Ted carried on as if I were the only mother in the world
who wanted to send her child away. My God, lots of parents send
their children to camp. It's *good* for children. 'Norma never
would have suggested it,' Ted said.

"In time, I began to hear some life-and-blood stories about
Norma from women who had been friends of hers," Sharon continued. "She was a very good woman, a warm person, they told
me, but she was *not* a saint. For one thing, she'd held a part-time
job as a dental hygienist—so she hadn't sacrificed every hour of
every day to her family. More important was the discovery that
Norma had sensed Alex might be a troubled little boy and had
spoken to a cousin about seeking professional help. So some of
Alex's tensions *had* existed before his mother had died, had surely
predated my joining the family. But Ted never told me that. When
I learned all this, I confronted Ted with it. (We were then seeing
a marriage counselor.) I honestly think he'd blocked it all from
his mind."

The marriage counselor helped Ted recall the good times of his
first marriage and the less than perfect occasions. She suggested

that Ted had to help the children feel comfortable with the image of their mother, but stressed he was to describe not only Norma's strengths but also her peccadilloes. He had to make Norma live, so she could be allowed to die.

Which is not to say the dead parent should be forgotten. The orphaned child should be encouraged to recall with pleasure (not with guilt) the relationship he or she had with the deceased parent and to accept with pleasure (not with guilt) the friendship and guidance offered by the stepparent.

SEPARATING FROM THE HOUSEKEEPER AND OTHER SURROGATE PARENTS

The marriage counselor also helped Sharon find the courage, and made Ted understand the need, to separate from the full-time housekeeper so that Sharon could declare herself mistress of the house.

When Norma died, it was immediately clear that a housekeeper would be needed to manage the motherless home. Mrs. Martin was hired. She moved in the day before Hope was brought home from the hospital. When Ted remarried, Mrs. Martin moved out but continued to come in daily to clean the house and help care for the children. Of course, she knew the children better than did Sharon, their stepmother. *Everyone* agreed on that, which only served to underscore the insecurity of Sharon's position in the home. Norma had been the biological mother; Mrs. Martin was the substitute mother. Who then was Sharon?

Women who marry widowers with young children more than likely will find themselves having to confront the issue of what to do about the surrogate mother who has come in and taken on the responsibility for the continued functioning of the family. The substitute parent may be a treasured housekeeper, like Mrs. Martin, or a grandmother, a neighbor, a favored aunt. In the long-running television series *"My Three Sons,"* in which Fred MacMurray played a widower with three young boys to raise, the surrogate mother was a colorful character named Uncle Charlie.

The remarried couple must face this question: is it helpful to the success of the new marriage to keep old Uncle Charlie on? Some husbands and wives will find the answer is yes. In a number of remarriages, the new wife is delighted to join a smooth-running family and is reluctant to disturb the established order. This is particularly true when the stepmother has a demanding career and is grateful not to have to become involved in the day-to-day running of the house.

Most stepmothers, however—even those who are working women—have found they do better to ease the family out of the helping relationships that predate the present marriage.

"I never felt the house was mine until the morning after Mrs. Martin left," said Sharon. "I'd lived in that house for years and here I was, finally responsible for seeing to it that the family ran smoothly. There were beds to be made and meals to be planned—and I liked it.

"Eventually," she continued, "we hired someone to come in two days a week to do the cleaning. The new housekeeper deferred to me as the woman of this house, not I to her, and that made all the difference."

If Mrs. Martin had been, instead, Uncle Charlie or Grandma, it would have been impossible to have continued the relationship as it existed for so many years and equally undesirable to sever it. The stepfamily must be aware that different responses are called for, depending on whether the surrogate is "just like one of the family" or, indeed, *is* one of the family. If you are the incoming stepmother, it is wise to keep in mind that relationships with Grandma will, and should, be maintained long after she has taken her apron out of your kitchen and gone home. The welcome mat must be left out and Grandma assured she is welcome *as a visitor,* but the stepmother must put on that apron to indicate her intention to take on the job of female head of the family, lest she be the one who is viewed as an intruder, knocking on doors for permission to come in.

We have focused, up till now, on a family in which one of the partners has lost a spouse to death. Let us now look at a stepfamily in which husband *and* wife have stood at the gravesides of their original spouses, and have then gone on to reconstruct their lives and the lives of their children in new families. In the process, they have found themselves experiencing more pain than they'd imagined and much of the pleasure for which they had hoped.

The stepfamily formed by the marriage of Judith Jacobs to Bob Kamen has been challenged by a wide range of problems, yet the couple remains firm in their commitment to one another and to making the marriage work. For Judith and Bob, "work" is a very active verb. When all is said and done, therefore, they consider their remarriage a success.

Life had offered few obstacles to Judith. She grew up in a lively, loving family, the only daughter in an academic household in which the children were nurtured and, in the proper time, allowed the freedom to stand on their own. Shortly after she'd established herself as a promising young historian, however, Judith met Mac, a young doctor, married him and went on to bear two children, Joshua and Eve. Joshua was four years old and Eve not yet out of the crib when Mac died suddenly, at breakfast, of a heart attack. In her early thirties, Judith found herself a widow.

Everyone marveled at how well she coped. Friends came up with a job offer: research assistant to a respected professor. Judith accepted the job. It was perfect. It called for her to work three days a week, leaving four full days to be spent with the children. In the next several years, Judith advanced quickly from assistant to associate to coauthor. She published articles under her own byline. She was asked to teach, and added a class—then two—to her schedule. She became very caught up in her career, an independent and respected woman.

She was also a woman who turned to marshmallow when she turned to her children. No matter the demands of her professional life nor the desires of her personal life, Judith placed her role as parent first. She would make up to the children for the loss of their father. She would see to it they did not feel deprived.

It didn't take long for Joshua and Eve to recognize their very considerable power. They took to making unrealistic demands on their mother's time and energy. Characteristically, she did not disappoint them.

During the next six years, Judith met a number of men. "Each time I came across a man I found interesting, I'd ask myself, 'Can I trust my kids with him, emotionally and psychologically?'" said Judith. "Unfortunately, the answer was no.

"People were always advising me to marry a widower," she continued, "which I interpreted as their request that I not take an eligible single or divorced man off the market. But I think I wouldn't have wanted a single man who had never lived with children. Nor did I feel comfortable with the thought of marrying a divorced man, someone who (for whatever reason) had failed in a marriage. I didn't see myself marrying a widower with little children either. I didn't want to raise somebody else's babies. I wanted to continue to focus on mine."

Bob Kamen met Judith's qualifications. He'd been a widower for three years when he met Judith. His three children, Jimmy, Gail, and David, were aged eighteen, sixteen, and twelve, all of them older than Judith's offspring, who by then had celebrated their tenth and seventh birthdays. Bob, a building contractor, was a moderately successful businessman who knew what he wanted. It was clear, from the moment they met at the wedding of friends, that Bob wanted to see more of Judith.

Bob speaks: "With my first wife, Jane, the children and I suffered through a long and painful dying. Jane was in and out of hospitals, and we stopped the calendars of our lives to be at her side. Finally, she died of the kidney disease that had wasted her away. And I became a wild man."

Where Judith had responded to widowhood by assuming greater responsibility, Bob abandoned his parental role almost completely. He let the children run loose, trusting they'd turn up at home each night. Often, he was not there to greet them.

There are all kinds of patterns that men who lose their wives fall into. By Bob's admission, "I became an animal. I had to have a woman in bed with me all the time. I'd had too much of dying. This was my assertion of life."

Bob went on, "I wasn't looking for a wife. Then I met Judith. She was the only woman I'd come across who didn't need me to lean on. She had her own life and interests. I proposed to her within two months. I told her, 'If it means getting you with two children, that's fine. My three kids are a part of me, and come with me; your kids are a part of you and I accept them as part of you.'"

Six months later, Judith said yes. She held on to her job, but relocated into Bob's community and Bob's house.

The day following his father's remarriage, Bob's eldest son Jimmy left home to become a "cactus child," in the words of his stepmother. "He's leading a life that's too rough to be flowery," she says. "He's been into and out of the dope scene, has lived for a while with a commune, and now he's resettled out West where he appears to be holding down a steady job at a ranch. I used to resent Jimmy a lot because of the pain he caused his father. We've now developed a superficial, respectful relationship. We seldom see one another.

"Everyone warned me, 'Look out for the daughter,'" Judith recalls. "They figured that Gail had taken over as the woman of the house and guessed she wouldn't be ready to relinquish that role. I came prepared, then, to have a rough time with Gail, and found my major hassles were (and continue to be) with Bob's youngest child, David." Gail hadn't ever taken on the mother role. She's very much her father's daughter. Like Bob, she too had run out to sow some wild oats. *If he can do it, so can I,* she reasoned. Instead of one of the children becoming the leader of the pack, each charted his or her own course. Each became highly independent. It was hard for each of them to accept any parental authority. Bob and Judith now feel this may be the major reason for Jimmy's having walked away from his home the moment it threatened to reassume a traditional family structure. He couldn't accept becoming *anybody's* child again.

It was David who suffered displacement as youngest child in the family when Judith moved in with her children. It was he who stood by to witness (mockingly, Judith thought) any scenes that took place between Judith and her own children. The family had lost its privacy, they were onstage and, Judith was hurt to discover, nobody was applauding.

Judith finds it hard to take any criticism of how she has brought up her children. When Bob or his children accuse her of having spoiled Josh and Eve, Judith responds, "Don't tell me how to raise my children. I did it without any help for a lot of years, and I did all right." She sometimes aches for David because she believes that seeing her with her children points out a void in his own life: where was his own mother when he needed her so badly?

"I was sewing on name tapes for Josh before I packed up his clothes and sent his trunk off to camp," Judith recounted. "David watched me for a while and then said critically, 'I had to do that for myself when I was Joshua's age.' I think David would have liked to have been spoiled a little. I think he'd like me to spoil him a bit now, to hug him and hold him, but when I come close, he pulls away. He's having a hard time deciding whether to maintain his independent stance and be true to the memory of his mother or join my family and become one of the children, which means accepting my authority and my love. When Bob and I were still considered newlyweds, David's way of responding to any growing feelings of closeness was to run away. One day, he'd be playing a game with Joshua and they'd be acting like two brothers, wrestling and squabbling; the next day David would be gone."

Once, he was off for a week. Judith and Bob became frantic. He had gone to visit Gail, it turned out, who was spending her school vacation as a waitress at a resort hotel. Then David came home. Bob and Judith no longer panic. David's flights are less frequent now, and he always comes home.

"Difficult children were no novelty to me," Bob notes, "but Judith's children proved to be difficult in a different way than I was accustomed to. My son David seeks attention by doing something bad. He acts up in school, and I'll get a call from the principal. Then I have to pay some attention. He runs away, and he knows I'll worry. I think I caused David to develop this mechanism during the years I was bedding around. It was the only way he could say, 'Hey, Dad, stop and look at me.' Now we have to get him to understand there are better, more appropriate methods. David has to learn he can try talking to me.

"Judith's kids, on the other hand, have to learn to shut up once in a while," said Bob. "When Josh or Eve wants to engage my attention, they will do so by talking to me—no matter what else is going on or who else has my attention at the moment. They'll tug at my arm if I haven't turned to listen to them the moment they want me. Or they'll insist on showing me something right then and there. They're a very verbal unit. Judith and her children talk, yell, confront, and hug one another, often in rapid succession. The thought of any physical violence is intolerable to them."

That is why the time Bob hit his stepdaughter, Eve, stands out strongly in the family's memory. Bob describes one of Eve's tantrums: "She was carrying on about something, her voice rising higher and higher, her tone becoming more and more grating. The children are overindulged; they sass their mother; they can be very insulting. My kids have *done* some pretty terrible things, but they have never talked back to me. I won't allow it. I asked Eve to stop—once, twice—and the third time I swatted her. I gave her a terrible black eye. That was the only time Judith threatened to leave me. It was also the start of a good relationship between me and Eve. We understand one another now. We even get along.

"Judith's kids do sometimes say, 'My own father never would have done this to me,'" Bob noted. "I tell them, 'Your own father would have been worse.'"

"There is a tendency for children to idealize the dead parent," Judith agrees, "and for surviving spouses to do so as well." She sounds again the recurrent issue in the stepfamily that has been formed following the demise of a parent. "This is especially true for very young children who create fairy tales because they have little or no recollection of reality. Eve was a year old when Mac died; all she remembers of him is what is told her, so I reconstruct little games they played together, games like hide-and-go-seek, but I also have to remind her (and myself as well) that Mac and I didn't always get along, that we argued, that we too had problems to confront in our marriage." She laughs. "For some reason it has become very important to me that Mac never liked my mother's stuffed cabbage. Bob, on the other hand, loves my mother's stuffed cabbage. There's got to be a symbol in there someplace."

Humor, respect for one another, and commitment to the marriage are seeing Judith and Bob Kamen through their second marriage. "A lot of the difficulties between stepparent and stepchild can be resolved by working through a better understanding between husband and wife," believes psychologist Janice Nadler, consultant at Thalians Community Mental Health Center, Cedars-Sinai Medical Center in Los Angeles. "If they work things through between themselves and present a united front, the children will acquiesce. The healthy part of the child wants a happy home to come to."

It was at least three years before the Jacobs-Kamen household began to resemble a happy home. "It has taken that long to merge two life styles," says Bob. "The children now relate better to one another than they do to either parent, and there have been some special moments we've all shared."

"I love it when my children call Bob Daddy," said Judith. "They did so right away. I felt good when I heard it. *I made this possible for them,* I thought. *Now they can be like other children.* And I love having someone to spell me. All those years after Mac died, I never had someone to rely on, someone to take some of the pressure off me. In a crazy way, although I took on a lot that I was not prepared for in this marriage, I gained more. I know that Bob is working *with* me, he's on my side, and it's a very good feeling.

"I think marrying our family has been good for Bob, too," she added. "It's extended his parenting. As his children grow older, he still has my children who look up to him. . . ."

Bob's thoughts were on a different track. "Every situation is different," he said. "There is no prize package. You have to work at any relationship, and if you're thinking about going into a step-family where there are so many relationships, you ought to know that. You should expect that there will be problems.

"I'm aware that the children will grow up and someday I'll be left alone with Judith."

He grinned widely.

"I can't wait," he said.

10

Matters of Discipline

The question of discipline rates high on any list of problems faced by families living in step. The merging of two sets of rules, two different life styles rarely is accomplished smoothly. Much more is involved in the issue of discipline than habit and expectation. Typically, members of a combined household engage in a struggle to determine which family is dominant; hence, they tend to infer a good deal from which family's rules prevail.

The blended family must not only work out its rules but its roles: *who* is the dominant partner, *who* imposes punishment on whose children, and in what manner? Are husband and wife perceived as a unit or as separate heads of two different households?

To better understand what is at stake here, let us look at the issue of discipline in a first-married family. Here, too, competing and diverse attitudes are likely to come into play as husband and wife each include in their dowries their own family history and sense of what is appropriate. More often than not, our notion of marriage derives from our family of origin, for this is the only family we know well enough to model our behavior on. Although we like to think we are different from our parents, we tend to replicate the patterns of their marriage in our own. (This is clearly illustrated in studies that find the abusing parent was once an abused child.)

The difference in values between husband and wife may not be evident until the marriage produces children. Then, signs appear.

The new father moves to pick up the crying infant from her crib while the new mother admonishes, "Don't go to her every time she cries; you'll spoil her." Two different attitudes.

The child grows older; a second child is born into the family. Father recalls his childhood home in which children were sent to their rooms when the parents entertained their adult guests. He finds he too believes children should be seen and not heard. A product of a less formal upbringing, Mother encourages her youngsters' involvement in many activities. She finds herself less bothered by interruption. "Children learn by asking questions," she declares.

It is not unusual for two adults in a family to hold differing views on child rearing. One hopes that as the partners make the gradual adjustment to parenthood they will find a middle way, one that throws off the family each was raised in and more appropriately reflects the mutual home.

Eventually, parents *and* children arrive at a pretty good idea of what's expected of members of *this* household, how deviations from accepted behavior are dealt with, and by whom.

STRESS IN THE COMBINATION FAMILY

The combination family is expected to make this gradual adjustment instantly! Two adults, both of whom are parents—although not to one another's offspring—will find they have some very different ideas about discipline. These differences *can* be worked out with time, understanding, and the best efforts of those who are involved.

"Sarajane is a relaxed parent; I tend to be more rigid," said Victor, addressing the difference between himself and his second wife. (Victor had three children in his first marriage; the youngsters live with their mother.) "What bugs one of us doesn't disturb the other. Neither of us is right or wrong, but it shortly became clear to both of us we had to find *some* way to handle the differences.

"Sarajane's two children would stay up till all hours," Victor offered as an example. "As a divorced working mother, she liked to have the children keep her company in the evenings, and so she was lenient about bedtimes. The fact that the kids were up late really bothered me. I need some time to be alone or with my wife in the evening. I found myself getting very irritable, snapping at the children and at Sarajane.

"Sarajane and I discussed the matter, and a new bedtime was set. It's later than I would have liked, but it's firm, so the children know it's important in *this* family.

"You can't just grumble to yourself," said Victor. "You've got to bring the matters up and try to work out some sort of compromise."

Those who work with remarried families agree that constant and open communication between the partners about the children is essential. Psychologist Janice Nadler advises stepmothers, "If you want support from your husband, *ask* for it, and be specific. It's better to ask for help than to rely on mind reading, and then be disappointed when your partner doesn't do as you'd like."

It is also better for the husband and wife to present a united front. When they sense there is a disagreement, children will play one parent off against the other. This is especially true in the stepfamily, in which the youngsters believe they have something important to gain by undermining the role and the authority of the nonparent.

"Open communication" means a good deal more than agreement on how to handle Janie's school problems (take away her TV privileges or sit down for a heart-to-heart discussion?). In the stepfamily, it means there must be no covert messages by the parent that the nonparent is to remain uninvolved in the actual raising of the children. The issue must be faced: is the real parent prepared to *share* his children?

I stress *sharing* because some parents are totally controlling of their own children, while others, having found someone to take over the tasks of parenting, will sigh with relief as they give over total responsibility to a spouse. This is often the case when a man who had been the single parent remarries. He can now emerge as the benevolent parent, leaving the stepmother to play the despot. Psychologist James Meltzer observes, "There is an enormous pull in stepfamilies for polarization, where one partner becomes the good parent and the other partner becomes the bad parent. It has to be brought out on the table and discussed."

Generally speaking, adjustments in the full-time stepfamily are more easily made where young children are involved. Not surprisingly, adolescents are least likely to accept the dictates of a new parent. Said one stepfather, "There have been times when my older stepchildren have questioned my authority. They've said, 'You're not my father. You don't have the right to tell me what to do.' They don't pull this unless they're very obstinate and angry. Although I'm inwardly hurt, I generally tell them, 'Like hell I don't have the right. . . .' In their mother's eyes, my status as a parent is clear. She knows I was committed to be a parent from the start of our relationship."

"WHAT'S MINE IS MINE"

Many stepparents find themselves on much less solid ground. Not only is their status as a parent unclear to the partner who is the real parent, but they fail to perceive themselves in the parenting role.

A stepfather speaks: "My wife's attitude toward her children is one of unconditional love. For the stepparent, there is more of a judgmental relationship implicit. The degree to which I feel I can love my stepchildren is based conditionally on how the children behave. Similarly, the degree to which they love me is based in large part on how they see my behavior."

Where love is conditional, the stepparent feels his every word is being judged—by stepchildren, mate, and by himself.

A woman in a his-and-hers family: "There definitely *is* a problem, even if you do impose discipline in what you think is an evenhanded manner. The 'real parent' is listening and judging: *Don't you think you're a little too hard on my children and too protective of your own?"*

The stepchild is listening, too. Negative feelings expressed by the nonparent are more threatening to the stepchild who senses the whole relationship is on the line. Another remarried parent declares: "My fifteen-year-old daughter will not accept the authority of her stepfather. If he doesn't wholeheartedly approve of anything she does, she interprets his comments as negative. From her own father, she sees criticism as caring."

This woman has "solved" the problem by setting rules and meting out punishment for her own children; her husband has assumed the same role with regard to his son.

Many combined families fall into this pattern. In doing so, they perpetuate the division between the families. What they are saying, in effect, is, "What's mine is mine and what's yours is yours" —negating the possibility of the children becoming "ours."

The fifteen-year-old is correct. When it is well intentioned, criticism *is* caring. Given time, she might have come to realize this was true not only in her relationship with her father but also in dealings with her stepfather. *If* her stepfather, with the agreement (and encouragement) of her mother, had not abandoned his efforts to reach her.

A few words about "encouragement." Many parents in a remarried home will express the wish to have their new spouse become "just like a real parent" to their children, while at the same time their actions sabotage the stepparent's efforts to form a familial relationship. It isn't easy to sort out the feelings. The real parent both wants, and is jealous of, closeness between his or her children and the new mate. The parent may convey this by statement or by inference. Either way, the message is clear.

THE IMPORTANCE OF ASSERTING AUTHORITY

The incoming adult is therefore cautious about overstepping bounds. This person wonders: how much of a parent can I be without intruding on the real parent? (This concern is stronger in remarriage following divorce than in those entered into after a real parent has died.) Surrogate parents who have asserted their authority, however, speak of those incidents as major breakthroughs to better understanding between them and their stepchildren.

Listen to Amos McFadden, thirty-six, noncustodial father of two, at present husband of Lynn and resident stepfather to her three children, two boys and a girl: "Discipline in the stepfamily is a thorny issue. Lynn was typical of most single parenting mothers in that she was *very* permissive. When it comes to matters of discipline—the deference due parents, the obligations of the children in the home—you might say I belong to the old school. I've been strict with my kids, but I'm not that way with Lynn's children. Still, a lot of the things they did got under my skin. Early on, I had to decide if it was worth breaking up our marriage over dirty dishes being left on the table. I'd say, 'I don't clean up after the children.' Lynn's attitude was, 'It's easier to do it for them than to nag them to clean up.' I had to change my attitude.

"In general, I deferred to Lynn. She's a strong woman, and I figured these were her children. I tried to remain aloof from the family business. I tried to withdraw, but that didn't work. It placed an unfair burden on Lynn. Then one day Lynn's older son, Bill, threw a marble ash tray at his sister. It grazed her forehead. I was furious. I went up to his room and I laced into him *as if he were my own*. That broke the ice. Up till then he had been testing me. Finally, I had passed. I'm no longer a guest in the family. I've become kind of a father."

Listen to Cyril, forty-six, whose grown children drift in and out of the home he now shares with Barbara, thirty-seven, and her youngsters, Greg, seventeen, and Glynnis, fifteen: "I'd been living with Barbara for about a year and had a rather loose relationship with her children. Our comings together were sometimes pleasant and sometimes not. Basically, I thought of them as Barbara's children. The night I recall is one in which Glynnis and a friend went to the park. It grew late. Barbara and I grew worried. We went out to look for the girls and returned home an hour later. Our search had been unsuccessful.

"When Glynnis finally breezed in, at around midnight, I took her into the bedroom and I walloped her. Generally, I'm not a spontaneous person, but I suddenly realized that I cared about Glynnis *as my own child*—I was frightfully concerned—and so I reacted spontaneously. I don't think Glynnis holds that night against me. I think she was delighted. I should tell you the next morning was the first time she called me Dad. The title has stuck."

Listen again to Marilyn Krogh, whose family of eight (two adults, three of his children, three of hers) we met in our discussion of the combination family: "When it came to discipline, William and I bounced around a lot. Sometimes, one of us was disciplining the other's child, and the *real* parent thought the non-parent was too harsh. So we decided, 'Okay, we'll each handle our own.'

"That didn't work out because the children were looking to see how consistent we'd be in the rules we set and in their enforcement. So we decided we'd consult with one another before we would impose any punishment. There are *six* children in this house. We'd have to spend all our time consulting! The two youngest were the most vulnerable. One cross word from me and William's daughter would whimper. Two words and she'd cry. So one day, after three or more words had her wailing away, I held Michelle closely and I told her calmly, 'Listen, Michelle, I love you and that's why I will yell at you—because I care.' I think she understands now. It's true, you know. You have to care about someone to fight with her."

In his book, *How to Discipline—with Love,* Dr. Fitzhugh Dodson writes about the stepfamily: "Some parents will effectively discipline their own children. I think this is a mistake. You want to start out *slowly* disciplining your stepchildren, but you are abdicating your position as an authority in the home if you leave all of the disciplining to your spouse."

He cautions, "Remember that emotional rapport is an absolute prerequisite to discipline. Your first job as a stepparent is to build emotional rapport with your stepchildren. Remember also not to confuse *discipline* with *punishment.* Reward positive behavior and use a variety of techniques to discourage misbehavior."

REWARD POSITIVE BEHAVIOR

We sometimes get so carried away on the issue of imposing sanctions on youngsters that we forget to apply a pat on the back when that is well deserved. Marie Shukaitis, an instant parent who is also coleader of a stepparents' workshop, noted that in the early stages of their marriage, she and her husband were so involved with one another, "We didn't take time out for small talk with the children, for praise—but we would *always* take the time to reprimand. The children learned they could always command our attention by negative acts. We learned from experience, which I now pass on to others. It is important to see that children don't have to set up negative situations in order to get attention."

TECHNIQUES TO DISCOURAGE MISBEHAVIOR

Recognizing that there is no universal style of discipline, counselor Thelma Kaplan, nevertheless, asks blended families to be consistent, to decide: is this an authoritarian or more democratic household? "Children cannot be expected to conform to the rules of the house if they don't know what those rules are. So make the rules clear," she admonishes.

Working with his-and-hers households, Kaplan goes further. "In co-operation with the entire family, I set up a list of rules and regulations," said the marriage, family, and child counselor. "This sees to it that no child or group of children gets the dirty work, while others get away free and clear. The list is posted in some prominent place, like the refrigerator door."

This itemization of responsibilities and regulations works even in families in which one set of children live at home and the other spouse's children visit. It helps visiting children know what is expected of them, and spares the stepparent's having to lay down the law emotionally (or suffer in silence) each time the youngsters arrive.

DISCIPLINE IN THE PART-TIME FAMILY

As was noted in the discussion on the visiting stepchild, it is harder for both parent and stepparent to impose discipline on drop-in children than it is for them to set expectations for youngsters who reside in the home. In particular, the spouse of the part-time parent must become reconciled to having a lesser role to play. The stepparent *can* control what is acceptable in his or her own household, but cannot hope to have great impact on the general behavior of the youngsters.

An interesting finding by Janice Nadler, reported in her doctoral dissertation on *The Psychological Stress of the Stepmother*, is that part-time stepmothers have more conflict with *younger* children than do either full-time stepmothers or natural mothers. She sees this as "a reaction to the greater demands attendant upon a stepmother who receives visits from a child below the age of twelve.

"It is conceivable," Dr. Nadler hypothesizes, "that the part-time stepmother feels that a younger child is in more need of upbringing, training, and parental guidance than an older child, but because the stepmother is unsure of the degree to which she should become involved in the parenting role, she inhibits her natural desire to guide and rear her stepchild and so she experiences more conflict."

Quite a few of the stepmothers interviewed by Dr. Nadler complained that they were excluded from the decisions made concerning their stepchildren and so felt they had responsibility but no authority.

The shorthand expression of this sentiment was made, time and again, by countless stepmothers who admitted in frustration: "I feel like a maid."

Nadler concludes, "It is [my] belief that a stepmother who is not sanctioned by her husband to participate in child-rearing will be uncertain of her place in the family."

Nadler's advice to the nonparent in disciplining other people's children is clear: "Don't use third parties. Don't tell the parent to tell the child. . . . Instead, work out any problems with the child directly."

This seems to be true as well for stepfathers in dealing with their wives' children. We heard it from Amos McFadden; we heard it from Cyril; I heard it from a majority of men who live in households with children who are not their own. When they let down the barriers, when they take an active hand in rewarding and disciplining their stepchildren, they cease to be outsiders and become someone who is much more like a father.

Learning how to communicate feelings to the children and to give them an opportunity to express their concerns is important. Together, members of the remarried family may be able to generate ideas about solutions and come to a mutual decision. "If a child feels he's part of the decision process," advises Dr. Nadler, "he'll be more likely to follow through."

The same counsel can be applied to the parent in relating to his other spouse. If the stepparent feels a part of the decision-making process, she or he will be more likely to accept the responsibility of child care in return for full citizenship in the family.

11

Many Things You Might Wish to Disregard About S-E-X But You Really Ought to Consider

Sexuality is a pervasive force in every relationship. In the blended family, with its complex and multifaceted relationships, the impact of this force is considerable. Not only are husband and wife adjusting to a new sexual relationship, but so are the children: to their own parents, their stepparents and—where there are incoming stepsiblings—to the other youngsters who invade the home.

Age and *sex* are important variables in understanding the nature of the sexual problems that may manifest themselves in the stepfamily. It is generally acknowledged, for example, that during adolescence mother-daughter relationships are at their lowest ebb. If a stepfather enters the scene at this time, don't be surprised if problems greet him at the threshold. His wife's daughter now has the opportunity to extend the competition with her mother into sexual areas in a manner in which she could not have competed for the attention of her own father. To a great extent, the incest taboo does not apply, leaving daughter with an option to engage in sexual games playing.

She does not always play alone.

GAMES BLENDED FAMILIES PLAY

Paul is forty years old, slim, handsome, father of a sixteen-year-old son and a daughter, fourteen, both of whom live with their mother. Paul and his current wife, Sandy, also forty, make their home with her three children, the oldest of whom is a daughter, Adria, described by Paul as "sixteen going on forty-five." Paul candidly states, "It has been very difficult for me to learn to live with a fully developed, very attractive girl-woman around the house—and my stepdaughter Adria is all that!

"When I started dating Sandy, Adria seldom was around," he explains. "She was up in her room, watching television or doing her homework, or she was dashing out with friends. I hardly got to know her. Then Sandy and I married, and suddenly Adria started coming on very strong at me. She'd walk over to where I was sitting and 'playfully' settle down on my lap. I didn't immediately move aside or nudge her off. She even went through a phase of finding excuses to rub herself against me. I pretended not to know what she was doing. The truth of the matter is, in a way I was enjoying it.

"Although I was, and am, in love with Sandy, I was flattered and a little excited by the flirtation with Adria." Paul continues his recitation in a matter-of-fact manner. "Fortunately, Sandy is a rather astute, clever woman. She caught me up on it. I had begun to treat Adria as if she were older, a peer, not as my wife's daughter. One evening, I told Adria a humorous adult story (something I would not feel comfortable doing with my own kids). Sandy motioned me out of the room. She made me take a good, long look at what was happening. I'm glad Sandy spoke up before the relationship got out of hand. I'm not saying it would have gone so far as incest—if you can call it incest between two nonblood relatives—but it would have become a very uncomfortable situation."

Paul started spending more time with the other children, while he tactfully but firmly let Adria know he no longer welcomed her advances. She was hurt for a while, but eventually came around to accepting the friendship that Paul did welcome.

Much of the interaction between the heads of the household and the youngsters who dwell therein has to do with the sexual maturity of the adults, how well they relate to one another, and how well they understand what's happening in the home. They should be aware that remarriage itself leads the children involved to become more aware of sex ("Somebody new is sleeping in Mommy's/Daddy's bed"), more interested in what's happening between the two new partners, and perhaps more sexually competitive.

SEXUAL CUES

"If your cues from the children are seductive, then you have got to do something about it," counsels Eleanor Faulkner, who specializes in sex education and sex therapy. "The stepparent may not want to confront the situation, and may look aside. Indecision is action, too."

Some of the cues:

"She'll walk around the house in bikini underpants and an almost-bra," says Mike of his seventeen-year-old stepdaughter. "Then she becomes angry when she's told to put on a robe."

"My fifteen-year-old stepson will go out of his way to come down the three flights of stairs from his room to the basement of our house where I'm doing the laundry, to announce that he's about to go in for a shower," says Cecile. "What he's really doing is making the provocative statement that he's about to get undressed. He thinks that will excite me. It doesn't."

Another stepmother: "My stepson Tony is very attractive. He's built like a life guard. When we're at the beach house, I am very aware of his young, tight body. He wears those tiny racing trunks. I have to work to repress my sexual feelings toward him."

A stepfather: "I will grab my fourteen-year-old, boy-slim stepdaughter in a playful manner, just as I would one of my own kids, and she'll call out to her mother in mock seriousness, 'Mom, he's raping me again.' I think she really has sexual fantasies that I might do just that."

The stepdaughter who ensconces herself on stepdaddy's lap, the stepson who parades his physicality before father's new wife, are giving off obvious cues of sexuality at work in the stepfamily. The stepfather who grabs his fourteen-year-old stepdaughter "playfully" may not be raping her, but he *is* engaging in a kind of sexual play.

Sexual cues also are given by the grownups in the remarried family.

One stepfather complained to a support group of remarrieds, "My sixteen-year-old stepdaughter, with whom I have always had a loving relationship, is suddenly pulling away from me. I'm an affectionate, touching sort of person, and she and I always got along so well. Now she almost recoils from my touch. I feel I'm being rejected, and it hurts."

The members were quick to speak up. "At sixteen, your stepdaughter is not a child anymore," said one.

"Her pulling away is totally natural," offered another. "Sexuality at this stage of her life is real and frightening to your stepdaughter. She is naturally stepping back from the kind of contact you encourage."

In the situation laid before this group, the real parent should have been aware of what was going on. She should have questioned her husband as to the appropriateness of his desire for physical displays of affection from an adolescent. As is true for all situations that members of any family confront (and even more important in families in which members are trying to make matrimony work the second—or third or fourth—time around), open communication between the partners is essential. This certainly is called for when the challenge has sexual overtones, as it does here.

Counseled the psychologist who led the group, "You can and should show your stepchildren how much you value them. You can give love and affection through compliments and verbal support."

LOVE-HATE RELATIONSHIPS

Caveats against acting on one's sexual response to children are not restricted to the reconstructed household. In intact, primary families, it is not unusual for a parent to find himself or herself aroused by a child of the opposite sex, the more so as the youngster is seen as the developing adult. Growing recognition of the high incidence of incest between parents and children and of the sexual abuse of children bears harsh testimony to that reality. In the majority of families, however, years of familiarization lessen the novelty that enhances sexual stimulation.

But: "Stepparents and stepchildren are very 'new' to one another and are thereby more likely to be sexually stimulated by one another," observes Dr. Richard Gardner. "Accordingly, the situation becomes much 'hotter' and more highly charged, and the maneuvers to decompress it more formidable. *Violent arguments between stepfather and stepdaughter (as well as between stepmother and stepson) are one of the more common ways in which both may protect themselves from their sexual feelings.*"*

Thus Gardner draws attention to a cue whose sexual basis is much less obvious than those cited earlier. Frequently, bitter arguments between stepparent and stepchild are, in fact, love fights. This does not make them any the less serious or the more easy to take.

Gardner further makes the point that "sometimes the sexual titillation, rivalries, guilt, frustration and hostility produced by the sexual feelings between teen-age stepchild and the opposite sex stepparent can become so intense that the youngster's leaving the home (to live with the other parent or go to boarding school, for example) may be the only viable solution to the problem."

JEALOUSY

Several dynamics are at work in the stepfamily. Often, the incoming parent is jealous of the close relationship between father and his daughter, between mother and the son she has learned to rely upon between marriages or relationships. The stepparent wonders, "Where do I fit in?" And the youngster, depending on his age and closeness to the parent, may be antagonistic to the stranger who has invaded the premises and whom he sees as a rival for the attention and affection of the parent. The more intricate and numerous the combinations in the poly-family (as one writer has dubbed the complex family formed by the remarriage of at least one of the partners), the greater the likelihood that there will be misunderstanding and mistrust.

And there is jealousy of a sexual nature. Lest any stepparent to children who have not reached their teens read this chapter with complacency (*This doesn't apply to me*), let me hasten to point

* Italics are mine.

out that sexual rivalries do not begin with the appearance of the first pimple on the stepchild's forehead. They can—and do—manifest themselves earlier.

Nine-year-old Maura visits her father, Lester, and stepmother, Phyllis, every other weekend. One Sunday morning, the little girl scurried into the master bedroom and, whimpering over a bad dream, climbed into the master bed, snuggling for comfort against her father.

"Phyllis had a fit," recalls Lester. "She started *screaming* at Maura to get out of the bed. She continued screaming after I told her she was being irrational. She believes Maura was trying to seduce me!"

"I do, and she was, and she often is," Phyllis responds. Phyllis does not appear to be an hysterical woman. "I know feminine wiles when I see them," she says, "and Maura knows how to use them very well to get *exactly* what she wants from her father. 'Seduce' may be a strong word, but—yes—in a way that's exactly what was going on."

"Phyllis and Maura played one against the other and turned to me as an intermediary," Lester declares. "They were testing me constantly. I found it an impossible position to be in. If I agreed with either one, then (as they had set up the situation) I rejected the other. Not the *viewpoint* of the other, I should stress, but the *person* of the other. They became two women fighting over a lover.

"One day, when I'd had more than enough, I stood up and announced, 'I have two different roles here. Phyllis, I'm your husband. Maura, I'm your father. I will act to you in accordance with these roles. You two will have to work out your own relationships and not get me caught in the middle.'" It was the first assertive statement Lester had made, and it stunned both females into recognizing the game they were playing and how Lester was being used.

THE SEDUCTIVENESS OF VISITING CHILDREN

The story of Lester, Phyllis, and Maura leads us to consider again an issue touched on in an earlier chapter: the effect of visiting youngsters on the noncustodial family.

If children who live in the reconstituted household are poten-
tially seductive because of the closeness of the living situation and
the lack of familiarity that is assumed to exist in a family setting,
then those youngsters who only *visit* the remarried couple may
seem even more attractive—because they are less familiar. With
the passage of time, resident children lose their novelty. They
(and the parents and stepparents) emerge as total beings, warts
and all. Relationships are adjusted. Sexuality is played down as
family ties are built up.

Visiting children are guests who are called family. Often they
are strangers, not only to the step relatives but even to their
biologic parent—depending on how long it has been since they
lived together as a family and how frequently they see one another now. As strangers who sleep under the same roof, they may
find themselves provoked into sexual fantasy. As family, however,
they must honor the taboo against any sexual acting out.

In anticipation of the arrival of the visitors, and during their
stay, the tempo of the household changes. Eleanor Faulkner
points out, "The real parent may be more attentive to the visiting
child than he would be to a child who lives with him on a regular
basis. Such extra attention and attentiveness may feed into sexuality feelings—of parent or child."

The noncustodial parent may seek out more of the child's company, aware that he has it for so short a time. Faulkner counsels,
"A parent must be strong enough and psychologically sound
enough to give the child room for privacy."

When does a youngster need privacy? Whenever his or her actions tell you it's desirable. Eight years old is not too soon to help
the child begin to find his or her own world, to pull away.

ATTRACTION BETWEEN CHILDREN

It is not at all unusual, in his-and-hers family, for stepsiblings
to be struggling with feelings of sexual attraction for one another.
When their parents remarry, the children must rise to the challenge
of learning to live familiarly with strangers.

The nine-year-old boy with stirrings of sexual feeling watches
his thirteen-year-old stepsister scurry by in her underwear. He
finds it very provocative. The young girl might be advised to wear
a robe when she is not in the privacy of her own room.

But attitudes toward the propriety of dress and undress differ from one family to another. In the home in which two families merge, it is possible for each group to view the same provocation differently, one opting for a certain kind of decorum, the other for greater freedom and naturalness.

Blended families should confront these issues early on, before they are members of a common household, and lay some ground rules. Many parents who were relaxed in their attitudes toward personal privacy in their own homes, who do not see nudity or near-nudity as seductive or erotic, have found it the better side of wisdom to reconsider those attitudes when combining families that include young people of both sexes.

The stepparents' support group considers the issue of sex. A hand goes up, a question is raised: "My nineteen-year-old daughter asked her seventeen-year-old stepbrother to come into her room and rub her leg for her. She claimed she had a cramp. Should I be concerned about this?"

"One act does not constitute a seduction," responds the psychologist who leads the group. "If the next night it's 'Rub my ear,' then you'd better take a look at what's happening."

"What's happening" is not always an invitation *into* one's room. It can be a demand, from one child to another, to stay *out* of one's room, one's territory, one's life. The same kind of "lovers' quarrels" that can be carried on between stepparent and stepchild are even more likely to be waged between stepsiblings. Finding themselves thrust into the intimacy of family life, youngsters may find it difficult to sort out their feelings, including their sexual responses to the other persons in the home.

Pity the poor adolescent again. Struggling with her own emerging sexuality, she finds further complication in the availability of a love object—a stepbrother—whom society tells her she *must not* regard romantically. In defense, she does the opposite. She declares he is anathema to her, and the battle is on.

Time and again in the families interviewed, heads of blended households that included opposite-sex stepsiblings in their teen years threw up their hands in despair at the situation in their homes. Families are turned upside down by the struggle. Said one stepfather, "There is never a moment of peace between my daughter and my wife's son. Their relationship to one another is all shouting and doors being slammed."

Sexual energy thus redirected has been strong enough to break apart families who could not ride out the storm. *But the storm does die down.* As the young people grow older and find more appropriate persons on whom to bestow their affection, their dealings with one another may progress from confrontation to comradeship.

Some perspective is needed. "Let us not become so involved in the problems that may present themselves in the merged family," said one stepfather with the wisdom that comes of experience, "that we lose our sense of the pleasure of young, emerging persons about us. The man or woman who enters into a marriage that includes older children as part of the package has a unique chance to meet those young people not as children but as human beings. If the stepparent sees them as such, he or she may be able to sidestep the power and sexual struggles."

12

The Bittersweet World
of the New Extended Family

Sociologists point to the gradual disappearance of the extended family as a phenomenon of modern times. The multigenerational household, in which grandparents helped the parents care for the little ones and, when it became necessary, all members assumed responsibility for the care and support of the aging grandparents, has become a rarity. The meanderings of members of our mobile society have served to separate the nuclear family from the grandparents, aunts, uncles, and assorted relatives who in past have been its mainstay.

Having so stated, we should also add that reports of the demise of the extended family have been greatly exaggerated, for *a new kind of extended family is emerging* as a direct result of the increase in sequential marriages.

In families formed by remarriage following divorce, a minimum of three adults may claim parental (or parentlike) relationships to each child. Instead of two sets of grandparents, maternal and paternal, as many as eight persons may be considered grandparents if the parents of the stepparents are regarded as such by the child. It follows that there can be innumerable aunts, uncles, and cousins. Add to this tally stepsiblings and half-siblings; the resultant number of "kinfolk" can be overwhelming. So, ofttimes, is the challenging task of building the new family on a foundation that continues to rest on a shaky base of old ties.

GRANDPARENTS—FOR BETTER OR WORSE?

You or your spouse may have divorced mate number one but, when there are children involved, you soon will discover you have not divorced the aunts, uncles, grandparents of the first in-law family nor completely separated from the children's coparent. Like it or not, your ex-mate and ex-family stay on as members of your new extended family. The marriage may be over, but many of the relationships linger on, for better or for worse.

The attitudes of former relatives by marriage to the various members of the restructured family often depend on the circumstances behind the dissolution of marriage number one. Who was at fault?

For two years, Jerry carried on an affair with a married woman, albeit he too was married and the father of two. Finally, both Jerry and his inamorata walked out on their respective spouses. During the trying period that followed, Jerry's sister was very supportive of her sister-in-law Francine. The two women, who had always cared for one another, continued their relationship of love and respect. Jerry's children were somewhat comforted by the familiar presence of their aunt.

Several years, divorces and remarriages later, this important relationship remains firm. Jerry's sister has accomplished the difficult task of maintaining a relationship with her brother and his new wife while not abandoning his children and his former wife. When Francine remarried, her sister-in-law was her attendant, is now viewed as a favored aunt not only by her own nephew and niece but by Francine's stepchildren as well. "I doubt this could have been the case if my brother had not been the one who behaved badly," she admits candidly. "I'm glad Francine has been able to build a new life."

Francine, too, deserves to be commended for not succumbing to the temptation to visit the sins of her former husband on all his family, to cease to have anything to do with one and all. Because she was able to keep a clear head about the matter, she left the way free for the creation of a healthy extended family.

Where a son or daughter of the grandparents has died, the in-laws' feelings toward the remarriage of the surviving partner (and, by extension, their ability to accept his or her new mate) are likely to be ambivalent, even when they are kind and well-intentioned people. On the one hand, it may hurt them to see their son or daughter replaced as a partner and as a parent. On the other, they may also be pleased to see someone take over responsibility for the children, to see a shattered family made whole once again.

The incoming stepparent who is sensitive to this conflict can lay the groundwork for a good ongoing relationship with the grandparents by including them in family gatherings and keeping them involved in the lives of their grandchildren.

One instant parent who thoughtfully continued the practice of having the grandparents to Sunday dinner, who phoned the children's grandmother for insights into their behavior and their likes and dislikes, has never regretted the extra effort she expended at the start of her marriage. "I sensed that my husband's former in-laws were uncomfortable and trying to find out how they fit into the new family structure (I would be, too, were I in their place) and so I made them feel welcome and useful," said this stepmother. "I wasn't simply putting on an act for their benefit. In fact, they *are* useful, and they know it. Any time my husband and I want to get away, for a week or a weekend, his former in-laws are happy to come and stay at our home. They're anxious to help out, and it gives them a chance to be with their grandchildren, whom they love dearly."

Other, less fortunate stepfamilies find grandparental intrusion unwelcome, even destructive to the blended family. Following divorce or the death of a parent, it is not unusual for a grandparent, great-aunt, aunt, or close friend to move into the troubled home and become a surrogate parent to the child. This intervention is welcomed by the custodial parent who is delighted to have help with the burdensome task of single-parenting.

Sometimes, children move from their home to the home of their grandparents while the surviving parent attempts to reconstruct his or her life. When this happens, when the parent recovers and goes on to remarry, the children are returned home to the reconstituted household. The surrogates are expected to accept thanks *and* a drastic change in status with understanding and grace.

They do not always oblige. Resistance may range from mild disapproval of the new parent and (where the incoming mate brings along children of a former marriage) of the new family. Bitter and prolonged custody fights have been known to take place—the stuff that headlines are made of.

In one sensational court case, the grandparents refused to cede their right to raise the grandson who'd been left in their care, claiming the child's interests would best be served by his remaining in their stable home, which, they declared, had become the child's psychological home (and they, the child's psychological parents) during the long period when the boy did not live with his father. What's more, they disapproved of the "Bohemian" life style of their former son-in-law and his new wife! The judge awarded custody to the grandparents.

Although the number of such power struggles that make their way into court are few, battles between the generations are common in the extended life of the stepfamily. Grandparents and other relatives who may have disapproved of the divorce in the first place can be quite hostile to the new partner, and work to sabotage the marriage.

"You must say something about grandparental intrusion," declared Peter, an earnest young man, as I sat, listening to his anguish, comfortably settled in the small den in his cozy suburban home. "My mother and father are devout Catholics, both of them strongly opposed to divorce. Because I was the one who walked out of the marriage, I became the bad husband, bad father, and bad son. My own parents sided with my wife, a woman they'd never been very fond of, because they believed I had not lived up to my obligation to stay with my family—no matter that I, their child, was terribly unhappy, trapped in a marriage that was making me miserable.

"My parents constantly criticize me to my son. When I was remarried—by a judge—they refused to attend the ceremony. They do not visit my home, and they continue to fill my son's head with his father's sin. The boy is afraid to like me, much less accept as any kind of mother the loving woman who shares my home and has made my life worthwhile. To this day, my parents live with the hope that my present marriage will founder, and I'll return to my first wife and family."

Sharon, the mother of two, was divorced from their father David and is now married to Alan. Her former in-laws refuse to recognize any role for a second husband to the children of a living father, hence became infuriated when their grandchildren spoke of Alan as their stepfather. "There's no such thing as a stepfather," they told their grandchildren. "You can have a stepfather only if your father is dead. Remember that!"

"Is it any wonder that the children return home confused and hostile to me and to Alan after these 'heart-warming' visits with their grandparents?" Sharon asks.

Where the blended family includes children of each partner, the relatives (grandparents, also aunts, uncles, friends) can do much to aid in the reconstruction by welcoming all the new family members, or they can make the task of rebuilding more difficult by underscoring the divisions.

A remarried parent recounts, "When my children visit Grandma and walk into her home without saying hello, Grandma always manages to find some excuse for them. 'They're not in the mood,' she'll say, tossing off their rudeness lightly. But just let my stepchildren fail to acknowledge my mother with due respect and this same woman will comment bitterly (shrugging her shoulders as if to say, *What can you expect from such children?*), 'Sure, they wouldn't ignore me if I were their real grandmother. But I'm only a *step*grandmother, so why should they care how they treat me!' It drives me up the wall."

Discriminatory behavior toward one set of children can be harmful to the incoming youngsters, and keeps them from feeling themselves to be full members of the family they have joined. Such clear-cut partiality, while understandable, should not be allowed to continue. It is important for the heads of the new family to help the grandparents (and the sisters and the cousins and the aunts) recognize the fact of their favoritism and to explain why they must work to change their behavior.

Because the attitudes and actions of members of the extended family so strongly affect the well-being of the stepfamily, many therapists who work with reconstructed families advocate the inclusion in therapy of members of three generations of a family

and, when it is possible, of past and present spouses and *their*
mates. One caseworker reported a session in which twenty-seven
members of the extended family were gathered in one room.
Seven therapists participated!

If such measures (talking with family members, seeking professional help) have been tried and proven unsuccessful, husband
and wife in the new marriage will have to consider severing relationships with former kinfolk. Ties should not be broken lightly.
Children deserve to be allowed to stay in touch with the relatives
of both their parents. But the remarried couple must not be so
"understanding" that they allow former in-laws to sabotage the
newly established family. In such a situation, it may be best for
them to break their ties with the past.

WARM FAMILY GATHERINGS GROW TOO HOT FOR COMFORT

Family gatherings . . . holidays and special occasions . . .
birthdays . . . the times that make one think of home and hearth
lead the stepfamily to consider: whose home? whose hearth? All
the landmark occasions are fraught with tension, members of extended families soon discover.

"Participants in our stepparenting groups have talked about
'impending Thanksgiving,'" says psychologist Nina Cohen.
"That's how much many of them have come to dread the holiday."

Holidays are the worst of times. Which house will the child be
at? Father's? Mother's? Grandparents'? *Which* grandparents?
Some family counselors believe there is so much pressure built up
around the celebration of holidays, coparents would be wise to
allow their children to remain in their customary surroundings
where they can celebrate with familiar family and friends. Others
disagree. Holidays are occasions when the child has some time off
from school, they reason, and is thus able to spend a longer, more
leisurely visit with the noncustodial parent and his family.

However the problem is resolved, *one* of the parents will feel
the absence of the youngsters, and his or her holiday cheer will be
greatly diminished.

"We've been conditioned to think of holidays as times of family
gathering," declares Carol, a divorcée now remarried into a his-
and-hers household. "Intellectually, I recognize that my ex-hus-

band and his family are entitled to be joined by our children at Thanksgiving, but emotionally I'm devastated by their absence at our holiday table."

Jack and Joanne have six children between them. Three are his; three are hers. "Our basic rule as regards family functions," explains Jack, "is that I don't attend Joanne's family celebrations and she and her children don't go to mine. At Christmas, my children and I attend church and have dinner with my folks. Joanne's parents live out of town, so Joanne takes her children for the entire weekend and goes to see her family. The alternative, it seemed to us, was to celebrate *four* Christmases. Are you kidding!"

Jack and Joanne have bought domestic peace dearly, at the sacrifice of sharing special occasions with one another. But the plan they arrived at works *for them,* which is most important for any blended family. The decisions you make may be unorthodox and they may be questioned by inquisitive friends and relatives, but you are involved in making a success out of a life style that is still regarded as unorthodox. If the solution you reach is working, stay with it.

The most anxiety-provoking situations for the stepfamily are those in which members of family past and family present are brought together for the sake of the children. "I may choose to attend some functions where I know there will be members of my former family, and my present wife may decide to remain at home," said one remarried man, "but where the event centers around the child, there's no question but that we should all be there."

Even if it's awkward?

"I remember visiting my husband's two daughters, ten and thirteen, at camp the summer following my marriage to their father," recounts a Connecticut matron. "Not only did we trek up to Maine to see them, but so did their mother, who hadn't remarried, accompanied by *her* mother and father—the children's grandparents.

"To say we spent an awkward weekend—this camp permitted two consecutive visiting days, and far be it from any of us to leave sooner than the others—is an understatement.

"It was also difficult for the girls," she adds, "constantly having to make decisions about how to allot their time. The next year, we arranged our days beforehand. Their mother agreed to visit the girls on Saturday; my husband and I spent Sunday with them."

There may be times when the better part of discretion calls for the stepparent to remain at home. This might have been advisable in the camp situation just described had only one day been permitted for visiting, a rule in many camps. Rather than create a situation that tests the children's allegiance and makes a joyous occasion uncomfortable for all involved, the stepparent might wisely elect to stay home. It would be a good idea, however, for her to send some memento along to the children, something to show the youngsters she is thinking of them, *something to assure that physical absence is not misinterpreted as the absence of caring.*

FACING FAMILY AFFAIRS

The most uncomfortable moments in remarried families generally are connected with those occasions calling for the greatest rejoicing: the graduation of a child, the engagement party, the wedding. . . . Decisions must be made: who will host the party: How will the guest list be decided? Which family members will be invited? Which friends of which family omitted? Where there are to be ceremonies, who will participate and who sit on the sidelines?

Many of the guests will be seeing both parents together for the first time after a long separation, divorce, and remarriage. There will be awkward moments. Everyone looks to see what will happen when the former mates meet. How will they act to one another, to once mutual friends who have long ceased to be friendly? Will new spouses be deemed acceptable? Will they *be* accepted? How will they measure up to their predecessors?

"I felt like the other woman at my own son Justin's wedding," declares Judith. "Whenever my husband. Steve, and I are forced to get together with my ex, Joe, and his wife, Betty, at any celebration centering on the children (mine and Joe's), I find I am very sensitive. Betty often behaves as though she's the parent, and I resent it. At Justin's graduation, she told Mark, my younger son, to go to the men's room and comb his hair. And I was sitting right there! His hair looked fine to me, his mother. Betty carries the same surname as my sons, so people naturally mistake her for their mother, especially those who don't know there has been more than one marriage.

"A lot of photographs were taken at Justin's wedding," Judith continues. "They were candid shots, not posed. When the proofs came back (I saw them *for the first time* at Justin's home), there were many of Joe and Betty and—can you believe it?—not one picture of Steve and me. I'm sure the photographer *thought* he had been snapping the parents of the groom. I'm *not* a narcissistic person, but I wasn't recorded for posterity at my own son's wedding, and it is very painful."

So much so that when Mark turned thirteen and became a bar mitzvah (and Steve and Judith planned the party celebrating this milestone in the young man's life), the photographer was carefully instructed. Of the thirty-four pictures taken of "family," seventeen were of Joe and Betty, seventeen of Judith and Steve.

"I think it's significant that we *counted*," notes Steve.

The tale of Mark's bar mitzvah ceremony offers a classic example of how even the most carefully planned events can go awry. "Given all the relationships, Steve and I were concerned about how to handle this special occasion so as not to hurt Mark," Judith explains. In the bar mitzvah ceremony, an honor is conferred upon a few selected persons who are called to the platform to witness the reading of the Torah. Generally, these are the family members who are closest to the young boy.

"For my part," Judith openly recounts, "I did not want Betty called up, and I think Joe would have been unhappy had Steve been so honored. So I carefully named Mark's two grandfathers to be honored, because they deserved it and because there could be no controversy over this choice.

"On the day of the event, my older son, Justin, who can be very defensive of Mark's relationship with their father, suddenly became middle man. 'Dad should be up there,' he stage-whispered to me and, before I knew it, Joe *was* standing alongside the grandfathers. I bristled. What about Steve? Doesn't Mark live with us? Hadn't Steve become as much a father to him as was Joe? To top it off, Steve's daughter, Lois, chose that occasion to be petulant. She made it very clear that she was a member of neither family. She stayed apart and wouldn't even sit at table with us."

Steve adds, "I was surprised and a bit embarrassed when

friends from Mark's father's side of the family came over to me
and handed me cards and envelopes containing gifts for Mark. In
a way, they were recognizing me as the custodial parent. And I? I
was happy to accept congratulations from anyone who offered it.

"I really wasn't involved in the two-family struggle, not even in
my daughter's dramatic and foolish stand," Steve adds, "but I *was*
aware of Judith's pain. I felt sad that circumstances denied her the
enjoyment of what should have been one of the happy days in her
life."

"I was just thrilled by the fact that the whole affair was over!"
exclaims Judith.

There are alternatives to the "one big happy family" celebration. Where relationships between the units that constitute the extended family are strained, it may be better for each family to
plan its own celebration. Mark's father and his wife could have
hosted a luncheon following the religious service, for example,
with Judith and Steve holding open house later that evening or the
following day.

This arrangement would not have prevented the problems that
came up in connection with the ceremony (who shall be called up
and who remain in the congregation), but it would have permitted
each reconstructed family to bask in the pleasure of being surrounded by relatives and friends. Not incidentally, it would have
been kinder to Mark.

DUE CONSIDERATION TO THE CHILDREN

All too often, the heads of families formed by divorce and
remarriage are so caught up in their own feelings and in a continuation of the hostilities that broke up the marriage that they lose
sight of the feelings of the children. Is this not the day the child
has been looking forward to—a visit from her parents at camp? Is
this not the confirmation for which the young person has studied,
the goal he has striven to reach? Is graduation not an occasion
for relief and rejoicing? Is not a wedding a time for family to
celebrate a young couple's decision to venture into the precarious state of blessed matrimony? *Are these appropriate occasions
for parents and stepparents to step in and make a mess of things?*

To minimize the discomfort, experts suggest that as little as possible be left to chance. Nothing so quickly bursts a bubble as the sharp edge of bickering between two parents who no longer live with one another and with their child. You can help the child if you decide *before* the happy occasion how each special celebration will be handled. If ex-partners find they are incapable of coming together without carrying on, they should confer on how to participate in their children's lives separately. Who will attend ballet recital? Who will be in the stands to witness the Little League championship game? And if both families must attend an event, who will take the child out afterward? Such deliberation and decision-making could have avoided the following incident:

It was the afternoon of the day of Julia's high school graduation. Julia's father and stepmother sat to the right of the auditorium. Julia's mother and her lover were seated to the left. Following the program, at which Julia received the French award, Julia's mother, determined to behave well for the sake of her daughter, suggested they all go to a well-known ice-cream parlor in town. Julia's father suggested a steak house; he was hungry. He was sure everyone else would enjoy a meal. Julia's mother was concerned that her friend not be stuck with half the bill for the meal at the steak house. *The ice-cream parlor,* she insisted. Julia's father grew adamant. His former wife was being stubborn, demanding her own way. How well he knew the pattern. And how good it felt no longer to have to deal with it. *The steak house!*

Julia solved the problem in her own way, "Everybody," she said, eying the assembled crew, "thank you for coming." And off she went to celebrate (it matters not where) with her boy friend and his family, leaving both parents and their partners without a meal but with a lot of egg on their faces.

13

Remarriage in Maturity

There is a saying, "Little children, little problems; big children, big problems." Many men and women who marry in their middle or senior years, following a divorce or the death of a spouse, find this aphorism all too true.

Couples who consider marriage after the children are grown might expect to be unburdened by the issues that so often weigh down the stepfamily. For them, the challenge of stepparenthood has nothing to do with raising youngsters in the home (although it may greatly involve sons and daughters who visit—or refuse to). These men and women have seen their offspring to adulthood, they may have ushered their own sons and daughters down the aisle, and now they themselves are preparing to stand at the altar.

Do the children give their parents away with pleasure? Not always. Many an older parent finds that the children are offended by the fact of their dating, see it as a betrayal of the memory of the deceased. "You sound like you're bragging," a thirty-year-old woman accused her fifty-two-year-old mother on hearing that the woman, widowed for a year, had a date with a gentleman. "I think it's obscene."

"My daughter is unwilling to have me go out with *anybody*," this woman remarked. "Imagine what her reaction will be if I remarry. And believe me—I'm looking!"

Then there are the sons and daughters who favor a parent's remarriage in principle, but are displeased with the selection of a particular marital partner.

"I was delighted when my father announced he was going to marry again," protested Mavis, a handsome and accomplished woman in her middle years. "My father was sixty-two at the time, a widower, and I was twenty-seven, divorced, and back home living with him. I was pleased he'd found someone for companionship and glad to relinquish the responsibility of keeping house for him. While the idea of his remarrying was fine, the reality of his choice was quite another matter.

"My own mother had been erudite, gracious, a woman of taste and talent," Mavis declared. "Freda, my stepmother, was a hardworking, well-meaning soul who was a good enough person, but certainly was not the kind of individual with whom I was comfortable. What I really resented was that she went around introducing herself to everyone as my mother. Can you imagine?" Mavis's voice rose several octaves. "I *never* would have chosen that woman for my mother—and *certainly* I wouldn't have selected her for my father!

"I moved out."

"I wouldn't have chosen her . . . or him. . . ." That statement was repeated time and again by persons who became stepchildren in adulthood. The grown child sits in judgment of a parent's choice of mate; he or she can make that judgment very clear in ways that cause pain and tension in the home of the remarried couple.

"I know Mavis always has looked down on me," said Freda, her stepmother, in a separate interview. Freda is pleasant-looking, soft-spoken, the kind of woman one often finds working behind the jewelry counter in a moderate-priced department store—something Freda might have had to do had she not met and married Mavis's father. "Her father and I have been married for fifteen years now, and Mavis still barely tolerates me when she visits. It hurts. Oh, she's never come out and said anything bad to me—she's much too cool and controlled for that—but she never looks me in the eyes when she talks to me, and she uses a tone of voice that makes me feel like hired help. She doesn't realize that her attitude hurts her father, too.

"For a time I so wanted to be accepted by Mavis that I ignored my own children," Freda continued. "I have three. I know it's hard to believe, but Mavis has never met any of them. My husband and I kept the two families apart because we thought we'd have fewer problems if we didn't force them on one another. Now, I'm sorry. I cut myself off from being close with one family and I never gained another. My husband has given me a good life and I'm grateful to him, but I can't say that either one of us has ever been really happy in the years we've been together. We might have been if Mavis hadn't cast a shadow over our marriage from the beginning."

Or, suggests a psychologist, if Mavis's father had strongly supported his new wife. Says this counselor, "It is just as important to tell a forty-year-old son or daughter as it is to make clear to a fourteen-year-old, 'This is my wife and you will treat her with respect.' The absence of such a statement may indicate that the parent agrees with his child's assessment of his partner and feels he must apologize for his choice."

"My daughter Sherry doesn't understand that a person has different expectations of a second marriage," explained Mimi, whose first husband had walked out of their marriage when their daughter was ten, their son seven. At fifty-five, her children grown, her career as a personnel director established, Mimi married Leonard, a widower. Leonard owned his own small printing firm, was semiretired; he is an intelligent man, but one with little formal education.

"Sherry feels I should have married someone more cultured than Leonard," said Mimi, "someone who would share my love of music and books, as Sherry does. She doesn't understand that one marries, at this stage of life, in large part to avoid being lonely. (For the first time in my life, at about the time I was introduced to Leonard by mutual friends, I was alone. Both my children had grown up. Sherry had her own apartment. My son was married, living in another state.) Sherry *said* she was in favor of my remarrying—but on the day of my wedding she got sick and threw up. At best, she was ambivalent.

"My daughter doesn't realize that, as the years go by, such things as trust, companionship, and mutual caring assume greater importance than common interests or—and I know Sherry is wondering about this, although she's never asked—are more important than passion. There is much to be said for uncomplicated affection.

"She also doesn't understand that a second marriage can be more comfortable than a marriage entered into when you're young. There's less jealousy, less tension, less competitiveness between partners. There may be more jealousy involved in the step relationships, however. . . .

"When Sherry comes to stay with us, which she does every once in a while," Mimi explained, "both she and Leonard are jealous of the time I spend with either one. If Sherry and I attend a concert (something we like to do), I know Leonard is unhappy. If I invite Leonard to join us, Sherry views it as an intrusion on the time we have together. We make a weird threesome.

"There's coolness between my husband and my daughter—not conflict, just coolness. Although I love her dearly, I'm happier when her visits are over."

RETIREMENT COMMUNITIES: ARE THEY CONFLICT-FREE?

Many remarried couples find that establishing their new home at a distance from both "his" and "her" family is advisable if they are to escape the pressures placed on them by the children. As couples reach their retirement years, this becomes possible. One marriage counselor suggests this may be a major reason for so many mature remarrieds' relocating to such adult communities as have sprouted up in parts of Arizona and Florida.

"We have a good relationship but not an important relationship" is the way one man describes his connection to his wife's grown son and daughter. "Because we moved to Florida, we see our own and each other's children at most once during the winter and for a month when we come North during the summertime. That's just about as often as any of us would want."

Out of sight, unfortunately for some remarrieds, does not necessarily remove them from the minds of the stepchildren. Some newlyweds find that the resources of their children and stepchildren are limitless. Battles can be waged effectively long distance —and they often are.

Karen would have resented any woman her father married. "As luck would have it," says her stepmother, Jessie, "I was the woman." Karen hated seeing Jessie moving about her late mother's kitchen, wearing a piece of jewelry that had belonged to her mother, or being accepted by couples who had been friends of her parents. What *right* has she to come and take over so completely, Karen complained to her husband, who refused to offer sympathy for her hostile position. Karen would not bring herself to address her stepmother by name—any name—nor to acknowledge the woman's existence. Most of her time, however, was occupied in thinking of ways to make *that woman*'s existence miserable, to break up her father's late-in-life marriage.

His daughter's attitude played a large part in Karen's father's decision to relocate in Arizona, where he and Jessie moved into a one-bedroom condominium apartment. Undaunted by the distance, Karen phones her father once a week. If Jessie answers, Karen's first words are, "Put my father on." If Karen's dad picks up the receiver, his daughter asks in tones loud enough to carry to the outdoor pool and beyond, "Is *she* there? Tell her not to stand around listening to my calls to you." Jessie's stomach churns. The phone call concluded, she invariably has an argument with her husband.

Karen sees dollar signs on the condominium, on every vacation her father and stepmother take, and pointedly asks her father about his financial arrangements: who's paying for the condominium; how and if the household bills are shared. (She'd be outraged if her father asked similar questions about the running of her own home.) What is foremost among her concerns? How the property will be disposed of if her father should predecease her stepmother!

"I don't think Karen realizes her father has much less money than she believes," Jessie told me, "nor does she know I gave up rights to my first husband's pension when I remarried."

STEPCHILDREN WITH MONEY ON THEIR MINDS

Money and its disposition are the cause of many conflicts between the remarried couple and the progeny of the first marriage —the more so when the fortunes of the two people involved are greatly disparate. The offspring of the more affluent partner are uneasy about (and often will work to thwart) the new liaison. Will the savings of a lifetime, they wonder, be squandered on a September (or November or December) fling? Often, they pressure their parents into having a premarital agreement drawn up to assure that the new spouse will not get rich from the marriage. Even more important, it guarantees that the children will not be left poor.

"I lived with Leonard for three years," said Mimi, the personnel director. "During that time, his son Stuart offered not a word in opposition to the arrangement. He was very friendly, very warm toward me until he was told that his father and I planned to be married. That put the relationship in an entirely different context. Stuart became very upset, even verbally abusive. Living together was one thing. As a man, he told his father, he could understand the desire to have someone with him. But why get married! At the very least, Stuart urged when he saw that his father would not be swayed, Leonard ought to speak with his lawyer.

"The lawyer advised Leonard to draw up a premarital agreement, which we both were to sign. Leonard's estate was to be handed over as a trust to Stuart—in effect, my stepson would now be granted power of attorney—and I was to agree, in return for a fixed sum, not to contest the arrangement or Leonard's will." Said Mimi, "I almost backed out of the marriage because of the lack of trust in *me.*

"I like to think I'm a good person," she continued, "that I can be trusted to do the right thing, and I was insulted by the insinuation that my behavior had to be dictated, and then signed, sealed, and guaranteed.

"Although I've a good job, I have never managed to save any money," Mimi explained. "Everything I earned went to support my children. My former husband never contributed a dime. I still don't have any idea of how well off Leonard is, but it's quite clear that he is very comfortable. . . . I asked Leonard what would happen to me if he became ill. I'd be willing to give up my job to care for him—I see that as a wife's responsibility—but if I did that, I'd be giving up my income and reducing the amount of the pension that would someday come due. How would I live? Who would take care of me? He hadn't thought about that part of it, Leonard said.

"I did not sign any financial agreement and, as you know, Leonard and I *were* married, which has led to a good deal of coolness between my stepson and me. Unfortunately, the incident also has had the effect of leaving Leonard and me unable to talk about money at all."

IF YOU THINK THERE MAY BE PROBLEMS

Couples who think about remarrying should talk about finances and get matters straight between them before they make out the check to pay for the marriage license. "Underline that statement," advised one attorney who specializes in matrimonial law. "There is nothing so disturbing as seeing two people in their seventies getting a divorce two years after their marriage, yet it happens all the time because the partners were not honest with one another at the time of the marriage." She adds, "If a couple can't work financial matters out before they are married, then they shouldn't get married. This is not pleasant advice, but it is unfortunately necessary because money becomes such a great problem for so many older persons."

Where each of the remarrying partners is living on a limited income, both may have to pool their resources to meet the expenses of their joint household. Generally speaking, this is not the kind of situation that engenders distrust nor does such a union cause the stepchildren to come running.

Where there *is* concern is with those remarriages in which one of the parties has a good deal of money and wishes to leave most of it to his or her children and whatever heirs are designated. Every state has laws governing the right of the surviving spouse to the income of a deceased partner, generally in amounts ranging from a minimum of one third to one half the value of the estate, where there is no will stipulating the settlement of a greater amount. But the monied partner may be loath to settle so large a sum on a mate when the relationship is not of long standing, and the less affluent partner may be content to accept less than the maximum amount allowed by law.

In such a situation, a prenuptial agreement (also called an antenuptial or premarital agreement) may be entered into by the parties. Simply explained, this is a written contract, entered into in good faith, in which the spouse discloses his worth and agrees to settle a specified amount on his partner in the event that he dies or, in certain cases, if the marriage is dissolved by divorce. In accepting this settlement, the spouse waives her right to inherit one third (or one half) of the estate and states that she will not oppose the conditions of the will. This agreement is enforceable by law *if* there has not been misrepresentation of the estate.

A form of prenuptial agreement that often proves satisfying to many persons who marry in their later years is a will provision that establishes a trust (the principal being equivalent to a third or half the estate) for the surviving spouse, with the income from that trust payable to the survivor during his or her lifetime. Following that person's death, the principal of the trust reverts to whoever was designated in the original will.

What does this accomplish? It takes care of the needs of the spouse—the husband or wife of one's later years—without also providing money for his or her heirs; that is, it does not enrich the children and grandchildren of the survivor who has been the beneficiary of the trust.

"I had been married forty years, and my late husband had left a considerable estate," said Blanche, a well-groomed and obviously well-cared-for woman who, even now, it is clear, plays an important role in the lives of her three children and her several grandchildren. A year after her husband died, Blanche met Martin, a widower of moderate means, and for two years, as he relates it, they "kept company." Came the afternoon that Martin proposed marriage. Blanche agreed—on the condition that Martin accept certain financial arrangements.

The following day, Blanche got in touch with her lawyer, told him she was going to be married again, and asked him to draw up an agreement allowing Martin the income from a trust should he survive her. "But afterward," said Blanche, "whatever I had belongs to my children."

"Don't say you're going to get married again," warned the lawyer. "Wait until Martin signs the agreement. More intended marriages are broken up in lawyers' offices than make their way to the justice of the peace.

Everybody has a way of getting into the remarriage act. The children of the richer parent are busy protecting that parent (and, though many would not come right out and admit this as their motive, they're looking after their own slice of the family pie).

The sons and daughters of the less affluent partner want to assure that *their* parent is taken care of and not left without means in the later years when one is most likely to be in need of security. Tempers can run high as anxiety mounts. Blanche and Martin's story had a happy ending. Martin signed the agreement without argument. Blanche's children gave the marriage their blessing. (In private, however, they told one another this was not the kind of person they would have chosen for their mother to marry!)

If remarriage as a mature individual is something you're considering, and if there is any question about the economics of the situation, do not lay your account out before family and friends, nor should you solicit advice from everyone you meet. If you've any question about the financial situation in your remarriage, do consult a lawyer, one who is familiar with matrimonial law and, more particularly, with working out the financial arrangements for mature marrieds.

"People are very itchy about lawyers nowadays," declared an attorney who asked not to be named so that his comments not be misconstrued as an advertisement for himself. "There's been a move of late to be one's own lawyer, to purchase do-it-yourself law kits. And that's wrong. You can't write a prenuptial agreement on your kitchen table and expect that it will hold up if challenged. The law of wills and inheritance is very complex, and the reason it *is* complex is that it must protect people from all sorts of wrinkles. A lawyer who is knowledgeable can write an agreement that works."

It is also important that you talk matters out with your intended —clearly, openly, honestly. This may avert recriminations and law suits after the marriage.

GROWNUP-TO-GROWNUP COMMUNICATION

The importance of learning when and how to communicate, stressed frequently by stepfamily members and family-care professionals, is not confined to younger families. When blended families include dependent youngsters, the members must confront the issues that divide them, simply because they come up in the life of the stepfamily on a day-to-day basis. Many couples who remarry *after* the children are grown and gone from the home, on the other hand, try to sweep any step-related problems under the rug, which is easier to do when there's hardly anyone around the house. But dissatisfaction, like dust, has a way of accumulating. It is better to learn to air one's feelings, to discuss issues as they arise (and before they mount and become insurmountable), to communicate with one's stepchildren, one grownup reaching out for understanding to another.

"When I married Don," said Beatrice, an assured and well-spoken woman in her late fifties, "the contract didn't stipulate that I'd become an instant baby-sitter to my stepdaughter's children, but that is exactly what has happened. Don's daughter Mary has developed a habit of telephoning her father frequently to announce that she'll be dropping the children off at our house—for an afternoon or a weekend. Mary never asks to speak with me, to ask *me* if I'm free or willing and able to take the kids. Her father goes off to the office, and I'm the one who has to change my plans to be with them.

"If Mary plans to go away for a weekend, Don and I are expected to be available. It's as if she has no idea we just might have made some plans of our own. One of the pleasures of growing older is the ability to go places and do things without a great deal of preplanning. The children are gone and your time is yours to do with as you please. I've grown accustomed to freedom, and I resent having it taken from me so lightly.

"But I haven't had the nerve to tell Mary how I feel," Beatrice continued, "because I'm concerned about how she'll take it. I'm so afraid of upsetting our tenuous relationship, and of hurting Don. I wouldn't be at all surprised if Mary is walking the same tightrope for much the same reason. We should have been more open with one another, Mary and I. There is too much that has remained unsaid in our relationship. It goes against the grain."

Communication is not only a means of conveying displeasure. It *can* be helpful to express the positive aspects of joining a family that are often taken for granted by those who remarry.

For Beatrice, there is another side to the subject of her step-daughter's children. "While I don't like the cavalier fashion in which Mary drops the youngsters off," she says, "as though my being ready and willing to care for them is her due, I really do love the children. They are winning youngsters, warm and filled with joy. And they liven up the house. I love having grand-children. I love being called Grandma. This, for me, has been a big plus in the marriage."

When was the last time she told this to Mary?

Beatrice pauses. The question has taken her by surprise. "I don't think I've ever told her that," she admits. "I always assumed she understood how much I enjoy the children.

"I guess it wouldn't hurt our relationship any if I let her know."

14

Seeking Professional Help

The story that follows is not pretty. It was recounted by a woman
we shall call Elaine Johnson, who agreed to relive it in the telling
if it might serve as a warning to others who live in step—to seek
professional help when it is necessary, and in time. A stylish, attractive young woman in her early forties, Elaine Johnson was
hesitant, at times inaudible, as she called forth painful events
from a not-yet-distant past:

"After divorcing my first husband, I lived for five years as a
full-time single parent to our son Michael. Michael was two at the
time of the breakup. In the ensuing thirteen years, he has seen his
father all of three times! I have always worked, with the exception
of a brief period I will get to later, and it hasn't been easy for me
to meet my bills all of the time, but Michael and I managed to get
by and, in time, life became easier for us.

"I met Phillip, who became my second husband, through my
work. I was a division head for a leading buying syndicate and
Phillip is an executive with a department store chain. It wasn't
long before we were living together. Phillip was divorced, I knew.
He had a son, Ezra, and two daughters, Gale and Jana, who lived
across the country from us with their mother, Patricia, and the
man she had left Phillip to marry.

"Phillip spoke very little about his ex-wife and his children. I
will admit that I asked very few questions beyond the obvious
ones—names and ages of the children. Did he see them? Only

when business brought him to their city, which was not very often. What did they look like? He carried a photograph. They were handsome children, especially Ezra, who had large, dark brown eyes, good cheekbones, and a Kirk Douglas cleft in his chin—a feature I've always admired. I was content to let Phillip's past lie. That's the way I thought about it. Phillip, Michael, and I—we were the present, and it felt good.

"Phillip and I were married, and for a while it *was* good. We had each other, my son, Michael, now had someone he could look to as to a father, we lived well on two incomes, and I felt myself fortunate. Every once in a while, however, the calm was disturbed by rumblings from Phillip's first family. A letter arrived. It contained a photocopy of Ezra's report card. The boy, who had been an honor student, failed three out of five major subjects. Phillip wrote Ezra a scathing letter, demanding that his son shape up. Then there was a phone call. Ezra was a truant, his mother announced coast-to-coast; he had been expelled from school. Phillip sent a check by return mail, enough money to cover Ezra's tuition in an expensive boarding school.

"A second phone call interrupted our sleep one night. Ezra had been caught selling pot and God knows what else. He'd been picked up by the police. Phillip flew to Ezra, to try to straighten matters. He could do no less. After all, he was the boy's father. (About his daughters we heard not a word.) And finally, we received a telegram that contained an ultimatum: 'Either you take Ezra or he will be made a ward of the court.' We had twenty-four hours to come to a decision.

" 'Will you take Ezra?' Phillip asked me. I said I would.

"I tried to draw a pleasant face on the sudden change in our lives for my son, Michael. 'You won't be an only child any longer,' I told him. I tried to explain it to my boss when I quit my job. 'Ezra needs guidance,' I said. And I tried to make some sense of it to myself. Phillip was my husband. Ezra was his—now *our*—son. My obligation was clear.

"Ezra came to live with us. I should tell you that Phillip and I were of two attitudes about how the boy was to be treated. I believed we all needed help, suggested family therapy, at the least was convinced we had to find out where Ezra's head was at. Phillip believed Ezra had been rebelling against a stepfather who disliked him (this much *was* true, but as we later discovered, it was not the whole story) and that the boy should be given his head.

"Ezra's head was filled with schemes. I established a situation of trust only to find that Ezra lied a good deal of the time. He told me he was through with the drug scene and I believed him . . . until I came across a hundred dollars in the pocket of his jeans, and realized he must be dealing again. I confronted him. He accused me of spying.

"The situation in our home grew very tense. Phillip and I argued all the time. My son Michael chose to remove himself from the fray. He took to staying at the homes of friends. And Ezra? One day he told me I was the only person who had ever cared about him and he vowed to reform; the next day I discovered he'd taken money from my purse. I began to resent Ezra—for having been responsible for my staying at home, and for making home such an unwelcome place to be. And yet I also ached for the boy. I wanted to help him and wished I knew how.

"At this point, Phillip had begun to deal with Ezra in a physical manner—he actually beat his son once, in exasperation—and I was reacting to Ezra hysterically. Was I not giving him my all? What *right* had he to disappoint me time and again?

"As Michael had done, Phillip now took to staying away from home. He could not deal with the matter of Ezra, so he ran from it. I became the stayer. Ezra experienced rapid shifts of mood. I didn't know if these swings were attributable to the effects of drugs, but I was worried. The boy was warm and loving one moment—in his best of times, he was a hugger—and curt and abusive the next. I felt a premonition of danger. When Phillip was at home, I pressured him to see to it that Ezra received help.

"At long last, Ezra started to see a therapist. Sometimes, Ezra recited the name of his doctor as God. At other times, he refused to keep the appointment for his session. Yet with all that was going on, Ezra *was* attending school and maintaining decent grades. That was encouraging. It's strange, no matter how clear the signs of distress, one is willing to be lured by any shadow of a sign of security.

"Phillip was out of town on one of his by then customary extended business trips when Ezra ran away from home. The authorities found him in a neighboring city. He was almost incoherent. They called our house. When I went to pick Ezra up, the police wouldn't let me sign him out in my custody because I was his stepmother. So there I was, the only person willing to take responsibility for the troubled boy, but in the eyes of the law a nonperson. I couldn't locate Ezra's father. In desperation, I phoned Ezra's doctor and together we managed to have him released on the condition that we have him admitted to a mental health facility right away, which we did. Three days later, Phillip came home. When he learned what had happened, he criticized me for having his son committed. I think Phillip never reconciled himself to the stigma of mental illness in his family.

"In six weeks, Ezra came home. I was opposed to it. I feared Ezra would inflict pain on someone. His doctor said he thought he would not; his father said I was a hysterical woman. The first week Ezra was home, I returned from the supermarket to find that Ezra had dealt with his own pain in his own way. We came upon him in the kitchen. The gas had been turned on.

"Ezra was sixteen when he died."

"If I could do it over . . ." said Elaine Johnson, a wad of tissues now deposited in the ash tray before her, ". . . if I could go back to square one . . . what would I do differently? It is easy to say I would not have become involved with Phillip, and dismiss the entire incident. But I keep asking myself a lot of questions. . . . If I had it to do over, I would learn more about the marriage I was getting into *before* I allowed myself to get into it. I would have second and third thoughts about a man who did not speak of his own children: if past relationships remained so threatening, could I really expect that he was ready to commit himself to new relationships? I would have sought counseling, with Phillip, before we married. Phillip and I had been physically attracted to one another from the start. A professional might have helped us know one another better in other ways that are important to a marriage.

"When Ezra's troubles became apparent, I should have urged his father to seek help for the boy, instead of accepting Phillip's assessment that our obligations had been discharged with a sizable money order. And when Ezra came to live with us—a step I am not sorry I took, even though I also know I never should have stopped working—we should have all gone for counseling as a family right away. We would have learned more about Ezra and a good deal about ourselves. Perhaps we would have been enabled to develop strengths to cope with the situation in which we found ourselves. We might have been able to work together as a family. Instead, we fell apart. Phillip and I are divorced. Michael is in his last year of boarding school, and I spend the early hours of each day on my shrink's couch, before I go to my office, trying to make some sense out of it all. . . ."

SEEKING HELP

The story Elaine Johnson shares with pain is not your typical stepfamily saga. Thank heavens. But it serves to underscore (albeit very strongly) the need for those involved in reconstructed families to recognize that men, women, and children who have been through the trauma of family separation (be it the result of divorce or death) may need help in accepting and understanding the separation experience before they can go on to build new and satisfying relationships.

Dr. Richard Gardner is one of a growing number of family specialists who have become strong proponents of *postdivorce counseling*. Gardner believes it is important for such counseling sessions to include partners who no longer are married to one another and, often, the children as well—to help members work out their feelings about the end of the marriage. He recognizes the challenge, in many cases, in getting former mates simply to agree to be in the same *room* with one another, but believes the effort must be made if the family members are to go on to new situations, having mourned the old marriage. "That it's something that's rarely done is no reason not to do it," Gardner says firmly.

THE CASE FOR PREMARRIAGE COUNSELING

It is to be expected that families entering remarriage will face issues distinct from those confronted by persons embarking on marriage for the first time, issues such as those that have been raised throughout this book. And yet many men and women waltz into remarriage, refusing to face those issues. They do not prepare themselves nor—and this is of crucial importance—do they prepare their children for the overwhelming changes that are almost certain to take place in their lives. Family therapist Dena Whitebook cites as a reason: "The natural parents don't want to rock the boat, to lay stresses that might upset the marriage." This realization grew out of Whitebook's experience in working with stepparent groups. "When I asked how many of the group members had prepared their children for the new family," she explained, "I learned that *nobody* had. The reason given by each of the parents present? 'I didn't know what to say,' they all said."

Premarriage counseling can help men and women who are considering joining together in holy rematrimony to see more clearly what that challenge entails, and to plan how best to confront the issues. While starry-eyed lovers have their place in romantic fiction, in real-life drama it is the clear-eyed protagonist who has a better chance of living happily ever after.

Dr. James Meltzer, chief psychologist at New York's Roosevelt Hospital, describes the premarriage consultation process as one that involves *clarifying* and *focusing* on the relevant issues. "It helps the couple come to their own decisions on a more knowledgeable basis," he says. "In many cases, a couple of sessions with a therapist who is alert to the potential problems in stepfamilies helps prospective marriage partners who are considering moving into a step situation to clarify their expectations and fears. It can be extremely useful."

An example: "I saw a man and woman in consultation who were considering getting married. Both the woman and her prospective husband had children by their previous marriages. She was clearly anxious about getting married and seemed quite troubled and perplexed by her own hesitancy and indecision. The initial problem that they raised was whether it was better for the families—once the couple was married—to establish their home in the spacious ranch-style house of the woman or move to the community and two-story house in which the man and his children lived. Or, they asked, should everybody move to a new home in a new locale?

"As we spoke," Dr. Meltzer noted, "it became evident that more than a house was at issue here. Both the man and woman had been single for many years. Both had satisfying careers, comfortable homes, and reasonably good relationships with their own children. The woman, in particular, was very hesitant about upsetting her life style, especially as it affected her children. They had deep roots in their community, where their father also lives, and thus were able to maintain an easygoing relationship with him, which the woman recognized as important. If they moved, the visits to their father's home would become more formalized, with attendant strain on all involved.

"The woman also was concerned about merging families under one roof. Although both sets of children seemed to get along reasonably well with one another, the woman feared a change in this reasonable behavior if the youngsters lived together as a family. The man, too, had some concerns along these lines, but he was more optimistic that everything would work out well in time."

Dr. Meltzer explored with the couple why, if things were going well for them under their present arrangement, they were considering marriage at this time. Neither was sure of the answer. It seemed to the psychologist that marriage was not being contemplated out of a great personal need, but rather out of some expectation that if they cared for each other (and it was clear that they did), they *ought* to get married.

"We stopped at this point," Dr. Meltzer reported. "The couple seemed more relaxed than they had when they entered my office. They said they would consider the situation and decide if marriage was right for them *at this time.*

"I consider this a successful consultation," declared the consultant, "regardless of whether the man and woman marry. The couple came in to talk about the concrete issue of living arrangements. As we spoke, it became clear to them that other issues were involved. They left the consultation, I believe, better equipped to think about and communicate with one another about those issues. And the door was left open for further consultation."

If this couple should marry someday, the likelihood is good that they will walk into the stepfamily situation on a surer footing, having confronted their fears and decided that their relationship was paramount to all other concerns. The issue of where to live will become—as it should be—a less important concern.

The goal of premarital therapy is prevention—to open up the

issues that may become problems later and to deal with them so that they do not become problems. At the very least, it is worth considering.

Not every reconstructed family requires the help of a professional, either in the pre- or post-nuptial period. But many more families than seek it out could benefit from some assistance. Having experienced one failed marriage, the remarrier, as a rule, places great importance on a successful second liaison. (The failure of the first marriage can be laid at the feet of the first partner; *if I fail again,* reasons many a divorced person, *the fault may lie with me.*) It follows that many remarrieds will cover up problems that should be brought into the open and dealt with. Difficulties that are denied do not disappear. They have a way of emerging, and are often inappropriately expressed.

"I fought with my husband constantly over what I saw as his inequitable treatment of my children as compared with his son," said an articulate young woman in describing her his-and-hers household. "I even made note of the time he spent helping his son with homework as compared with—it seemed to me—the short shrift he gave my kids when they came to him with questions. I built the issue up and, I have come to see, even encouraged my children to bolster me by voicing complaints that I put into their heads. So we had a household in which the children whined and the adults fought—*always* over the children. My husband took to staying at the office later and later. I saw myself saddled not just with my two children but with my stepson as well. Who needed this?

"It turns out I did. The realization that I really wanted this marriage to work, and my husband's affirmation that it was important to him, too, led us to enter couple therapy where we were helped to confront the fact that we had been *using the children* to express our own doubts and fears about one another. I saw the close relationship between my husband and his son and wondered, *where do I fit in?* But I was afraid to ask that question, so I rephrased it: where do *my children* fit in? As I closed ranks with my children, my husband felt threatened. He protected himself by drawing even closer to his son. Once he and I realized we were using the children, we were able to stop. We learned how to confront one another directly with our concerns. It's been all uphill ever since."

How can the stepfamily know when help is indicated? This question was asked of several counselors, who offered guidelines.

"There are certain categories of symptoms that are recognized by therapists," said Dr. Richard Gardner, who breaks down his guidelines for the stepfamily under two major headings: *children* and *parents*. Under "children," Dr. Gardner would give consideration to three realms of the child's life: (1) *school* (where any change in academic achievement or social behavior can be observed); (2) *peer relationships* (Does the child seek out friends and is he being sought by others? Has he become a loner?); and (3) *home*. In Gardner's experience, home is the worst setting in which to judge a youngster's behavior, to draw the line between what is normal and abnormal. "For instance," he asks, "where does normal rivalry between children end and abnormal rivalry begin?"

School performance, he believes, is the best indicator. The experienced teacher knows what is normal for the group and for the child—when the child's behavior varies from what is usual for him and what is acceptable for the group in which he finds himself. You will recall that Ezra Johnson, whose tragic tale begins this chapter, began to draw attention to himself by falling down in his schoolwork, failing three out of five courses.

Not every parent who sees an F on a child's report card should rush the youngster off to a therapist. Dr. Gardner cautions, "There's bound to be some disruption right after a breakup or after a new family has been formed, whenever the individual must adjust to a dramatic change in his or her life style and relationships. Wait a few months and see if the problems are resolved. But where the acting out is ongoing, that child may need some help."

Dr. Gardner is strongly in favor of involving the family in the therapeutic process, and will often ask parents and/or siblings to sit-in on sessions when he believes the presence of others is indicated. "Where the kid's symptoms are the final manifestation of influences that are being built into him, simply to drop the youngster off for forty-five minutes or an hour one or two times a week

will not help the child or the family," he declares, "and I won't be
a party to it."

Turning his attention to the troubled adult members of the stepfamily, Gardner notes as indicators that help may be needed: (1)
frequent fighting, with extreme tension ("If you're *frequently*
thinking the new relationship was a mistake, you ought to see
someone to find out why"); (2) loss of sexual desire and
gratification; (3) loss of pleasure. "Obviously there are gradations
here," he cautions. "Everybody gets depressed at times." When is
depression a cry for help? "When it is ongoing, when the bad moments outweigh the good."

Dena Whitebook, associate director of the American Institute
of Family Relations in Los Angeles, California, and a stepmother
herself, sees many stepfamilies at the Institute and in her private
practice in Beverly Hills. "If anything," she notes, "members of
the stepfamily express fewer problems here than they do in other
communities, because every next-door neighbor is wrestling with
similar problems. Children feel less freaky, less different from
other youngsters. Even though divorce and remarriage are more
prolific here than in many other communities, they are more accepted here and therefore the familes are under less stress than
might be the case elsewhere."

"When *is* there a need for counseling?" I asked Dena Whitebook. She ran down her list of warning signals:

"When parents are so overwhelmed by problems, they feel they
cannot cope, it's a signal to go for counseling.

"When any family member is very depressed for any length of
time, it's a sign.

"When unreasonable hostility is the prevalent ·emotion in the
family.

"When any person (not just a child) regresses to an earlier
stage of development. (I've seen it happen with women [she adds],
where the new mate is viewed not as a husband but as a father
because the wife regresses to wanting to be cared for as a child.)

"When one spouse withdraws from his or her partner. (They're
unable to deal with one another and so the relationship changes.)

"When any individual's growth potential is threatened. (Take,
as an example, the child who always planned to attend college,

whose parent remarries when he is still in high school, and who soon after decides to drop out of school. This may have happened anyway, but the family ought to look at what's going on.)

"If the family feels they're doing okay, but they could be doing better, it would be wise for them to get some guidance," Whitebook concludes. "For this, the stepparenting groups are wonderful."

15

The Support Group:
A Shimmer of Light in the Tunnel

"Where were you nine years ago?" The woman's lament was directed to the leaders of the group of stepparents who had assembled on this crisp Saturday morning in October. "That's when I really needed you," she bewailed.

In the sunlit auditorium of the suburban center, some forty men and women greeted the woman's plaintive cry with sympathetic laughter. They understood her frustration. At one time or other, each of them had believed herself or himself alone in trying to come to grips with the stepparent role. Thus, they appreciated the woman's relief, even nine years later, upon finding herself part of a group whose members understood what she had gone through, what special problems of the stepfamily she continued to confront. Here, at long last, the woman could speak candidly to people who would not condemn her, who might even understand.

Nine years ago, when remarriage turned her into a stepmother, the woman did not find a support group such as this one. Indeed, there was no place where stepparents and their mates could share their experiences with others in like situations, no place to gain insight into carrying out the complex roles taken on by second wives and husbands. Quite the contrary, society expected the stepparent to possess instantly the nurturing know-how and the love that was presumed to come with the position. Having been dubbed a parent, the partner in a remarriage was expected to *become* a parent. Presto! Just like that. And woe to the man or woman who revealed that the magic word bestowed no magic powers. Stepparents came quickly to understand that the general audience had no wish to be let in on the realities of the step drama, and so they became partners in the deception. They wrestled with the issues behind the scenes, left it to others who might take on similar roles to discover the truth for themselves.

Fortunately, that situation is changing—but slowly. There is growing recognition of the stepfamily as a distinct entity. Several newsletters now exist that address the needs of this population. They include: *Remarriage* (G & R Publications, 648 Beacon Street, Boston, Massachusetts 02215); *Stepparent News* (Listening, Inc., 8716 Pine Avenue, Gary, Indiana 46403); and the *Stepfamily Bulletin* (Stepfamily Association of America, 26 Allegheny Avenue, Suite 1307, Baltimore, Maryland 21304). Books written on the subject of stepfamilies have proliferated as well. And manufacturers of greeting cards have added stepfamily messages to their reguular line. Some states even have decreed an annual Stepparents' Day; there is movement to make the first Sunday in October such a national day of recognition.

Nonetheless, among far too many members of the general community, the stepfamily is still viewed as a deviant (rather than an alternate) lifestyle. Or its uniqueness is ignored. As a result, far too many stepfamilies continue to grope their way in the dark.

The stepparents group is a light in the tunnel.

The primary role of the group is to provide support. By acknowledging that "we're all in this together," the group encourages individual members to open up, to talk of feelings that would be inadmissible in any other gathering. (Members seem to do a lot of nodding in agreement with the situations described. Wives poke husbands in eloquent nudging—*You see,* each poke implies, *I'm not the only woman on this earth who complains about feeling like a maid when the stepchildren come to visit.*) Men and women laugh and groan together, try to help one another by suggesting solutions to problems that have been encountered and dealt with in their own homes. But the greatest sense of relief, if truth be told, comes from hearing that others are struggling with problems that are much more serious than your own!

"Everybody doesn't have to go into therapy," believes Dr.

Clifford J. Sager, an advocate of support groups. "For many stepfamilies, just talking to others is very helpful."

In a well-run group, participants are encouraged to put their emotions into words, to talk about what is happening at home. Let's listen.

It is the first meeting of the group, which is co-led by a woman and man. She is a psychologist; he is a social worker. To get the conversation going, to open up the issues involved in stepfamilies, the social worker offers an example from his own experience. "My wife and I had lived together for a year and thought we'd come to know one another and each other's children pretty well," he relates, "and then we found that all kinds of change took place in our family when we announced we were going to get married. I learned that living together is *not* a test of whether or not a marriage will work."

(That the group leader is himself a stepparent is more the norm than the exception. Professionals attracted to this emerging specialty often are those who have experienced first-hand the isolation of living in a stepfamily, which has moved them to create community for others in step.)

"What happened?" asks a man in a beige sweater, picking up the leader's cue.

"First, the children changed. I guess they'd been content to let the affair run its course, but when they learned the relationship would be permanent, they began to show their feelings and their fears in a lot of little ways. My daughter, who was five at the time, refused to wear a yellow dress that had been her favorite. We think it was because my wife had bought the dress for her. My fifteen-year-old stepson took to staying out late, not calling to say he wouldn't be home for dinner. So we waited for him, and we worried about him. But when I tried to discipline him because he was making his mother very anxious, my wife stepped in between us. She made it very clear that *she* was the boy's parent, not I. I began to wonder what role I was to fill in the family. . . ."

The leader's revelation moves a green-suited young woman to speak about the situation in her home. "I know what you mean," she says. "My husband doesn't let me say anything of importance to his daughter, but he's perfectly willing to allow me to *do* for her. He and I have been married for five years; his daughter has been living with us for the past year and a half, after he won a long, drawn-out fight for her custody. In a way, I'm glad for my husband—after all, he has his child again—but when she moved into our home, I gave up my privacy and I don't see that I've gained anything in return.

"I try to be a friend to the girl," she continues, "but she constantly turns to her father for everything. I feel he doesn't support me. He doesn't want to share his daughter. For instance, I tell her she has to choose between another sweater or a new album—she's always in the record store—because I think it's important for her to face the reality of our financial situation (we're not made of money, you know, and my husband and I have to work very hard), and later I find that my husband has given her money for both. That hurts. I say she must be home by ten on school nights, and she goes to her father who gives permission to stay out till eleven. There's not such a big difference between ten and eleven when you come right down to it, but what *is* important is the fact that he has overruled me. The girl has no respect for me whatsoever. Why should she? I've become a nobody, a nothing in that house."

The women, as one woman, nod. "A husband and wife have got to support one another," one offers amid general agreement with this position.

The husband of the woman in the green suit speaks up in self-defense. "After more than three years of being separated from my daughter, I feel I must work on my own relationship with the girl first," he tells the group. "I have to get her to trust *me* again."

Having started on her diatribe, his wife is reluctant to let it go. "The girl has me up against the wall because she knows I can do nothing to her, that I am powerless," she goes on.

At this point, the psychologist intervenes. She directs the focus of the group away from the couple who have made themselves vulnerable by laying their situation before the assembly, and throws the general subject of discipline open for discussion. (She has intuited that the couple may need more help than a group can give, and makes a mental note to follow this up at later meetings.) "How many of you have experienced similar disagreements over discipline?" she asks.

Several murmurs are heard in response; a common chord has been touched.

"My wife is overprotective of her children," a man declares. "She coddles them. I believe in 'Spare the rod and spoil the child.' But she won't let me lay a hand to her children, not even when they're very fresh to her and she knows they deserve it, so I've decided to bow out of the picture and let her handle them herself. If they're spoiled, that's her doing. But I tell them what the rules of the house are so far as my space is concerned, and I let them know they're not to overstep my boundaries." (It is significant that this stepfather has established a boundary between him and his wife's children.)

"We used to have a problem with discipline in our home," offers a young man who looks not old enough to be a father, much less a parent the second time around. "We used to have problems about a lot of other things, too." He speaks with hesitation, and yet he is eloquent. "It got so bad I felt I was heading to the divorce lawyer again, and I realized that was the one thing I couldn't allow to happen. So my wife and I saw a marriage counselor who helped us understand we had to work out our own relationship, that we were using the children as an excuse not to confront one another. The counselor wanted to know if we were truly committed to this marriage. We didn't know the answer to that one, so we went home and did a lot of talking—*not* in front of the children—and decided that we were.

"Since then," he goes on, "we always present a united front before the youngsters. We may disagree with one another, but we'll discuss those differences in private. If that discussion leads us to change any decision we've handed down, we simply tell the children we've given the matter some more thought, and this is the way we see it now. We use the word *we* a lot. If the children see that we have respect for one another, they will respect both of us —including my wife, who is their stepmother. Things are so much better in our home now, I can't overstress how important it is to learn to talk with your partner before you can deal with the children. I think our marriage is stronger now than those of many intact, first-wed families because we *work* at it. And we've found it works *for* us."

There is quiet as the young man's comments settle over the room and reach the hearts of the group members.

The leader who has opened up the issue takes it on again. "It takes nerve for the natural parent to walk away and not try to mediate when there's an argument between his child and his spouse," he suggests, "but if you're the one who is the parent, you have to do it. You must learn to let your children and the stepparent work matters out." (In this manner, the group has expressed its voice on the issue raised earlier by the woman in the green suit.)

The members go on to talk of money, to discuss the strain that the "other family unit" (the coparent and his or her new partner) places on their own unit ("My husband and I vowed we were not going to let whatever happens in their house affect us," says a member, adding, "but it didn't work out that way"), to vent their spleen on the noncustodial father who does not send support payments with regularity, and on the natural mother for a variety of reasons. It often seems that second wives who find their actions compromised by the myth of the wicked stepmother have themselves created a stereotype: that of the vindictive, money-hungry, mean, and demanding natural mother.

"I've got to say something here." A tall, slim woman speaks up for the first time this morning. "I spent five years raising two children virtually by myself—except for holiday visits to the home of their father and the woman he left me for—and in those five years I was the burdened, misunderstood, mistreated, underpaid, and underrated natural mother. Last year, I married a man whose children live with *his* former wife, and I *now* find I've become the burdened, misunderstood, mistreated, unappreciated *stepmother* It's a no-win situation, either way."

Laughter. A good point on which to end the session. The members set a date for the next meeting. They rise to put on their sweaters and jackets, some continuing to discuss—in twos and threes—what has gone on this day, to exchange additional facts of their lives. The leaders ask for their attention once again. They want an evaluation. Did the group find this morning's get-together helpful? "Oh, yes" . . . "Very helpful" . . . "Worthwhile" . . . The responses are positive.

"What were you looking for when you came here this morning?" asks the social worker.

"That's easy," the congregants respond. "We wanted to hear other people's stories."

"In hearing other people's stories and in seeing others go through the same situations, members of the stepfamily stop blaming themselves for the tensions that exist in their combined families and realize they are human beings," explained Dr. Nina Cohen, who has directed groups for stepfamilies. "The cutting of self-blaming is essential. When defensiveness is eliminated, people in groups can and do go on to find solutions. Once they can state the problems, they are able to work toward building relationships."

GETTING ORGANIZED

In common cause, organizations are proliferating, groups like Remarrieds of Dallas and Duet Again (Des Moines, Iowa). In 1977, Emily and John Visher and Carolyn and Pat McClenahan (both couples in second marriages) formed the nucleus of what was to become the Stepfamily Association of California. The idea caught on and, in 1979, the Vishers moved to expand the idea into a national organization. Emily Visher, a psychologist, and John, a psychiatrist, believed both professionally and personally (between them, they had eight children) that such an organization was needed.

"We had a modest purpose—to change the world for step-families," says Emily Visher, only partly in jest, of their effort to provide national networks, support, and advocacy for families formed by remarriage. By 1985, the Stepfamily Association had grown to include sixty-two chapters located in twenty-eight states.

Although advocacy and public education are important aspects of the Stepfamily Association of America's program, the major focus is on expanding and strengthening local chapters in order to provide support for remarried families in communities across the nation. For some who attend the meetings, the topics that are raised have become familiar. They have worked out how to establish discipline in their combined families, for example, or they have established a workable means of welcoming the visiting stepchild. But at each meeting, too, there is someone—perhaps a husband and wife—who walks slowly, tentatively into the room for the first time ("It's not really because I need it; I just wanted to see what this was about") and finds—with a sense of relief—"It's about *me*."

"I don't believe most people need therapy," says Joan Howard, who has served as president of the California State Division of the Association and is herself a mother, stepmother, and therapist. "They need a good education as to what is normal, what expectations are realistic and unrealistic for a stepfamily. They have to drop the model of the original family."

In addition to stressing what is normal *for stepfamilies,* the groups often concentrate on the challenges faced by special segments of the remarriage population. As we have seen, the "instant parent" deals with different problems of adjustment than, for example, the father who lives with his stepchildren but has minimal contact with his own children. Depending on the needs and desires of the chapter members, special workshops and events are scheduled. One chapter has had a fine response to the activities it has planned specifically for stepchildren—where the youngsters, like their parents, are able to meet others in situations similar to theirs and share feelings—and fun.

The value of the stepfamily support group was brought home to me dramatically during a national conference of the Stepfamily Association of America. (The national conferences, held annually, bring together families from across the country. This one took place in Pacific Grove, California.) The day's program included workshops on such topics as Couple Communication, Finances, even Sexuality in the Stepfamily. The evenings offered guest speakers, games, a square dance. One afternoon was set aside for sightseeing.

Many conference participants, I among them, used the occasion to enjoy the scenic seventeen-mile drive along the Pacific Ocean. It was a beautiful, cloud-free day. At one of the scenic stops along the drive, I stopped to watch hundreds of seals sunning on some nearby rocks. A stepfamily drove up. They were easy to recognize. All three—husband, wife, and a boy of about seven— were wearing the Association's T-shirt, which bears the image of a kangaroo carrying a panda in its pouch. They also wore bright smiles.

"This weekend was the first time in three years that my stepson deigned to recognize my existence and spoke civilly to me," said the man. "I'm sure it was because of the warm feelings at the conference, the atmosphere of acceptance for all families, plus meeting other kids in similar situations." He put his arm around the boy's small shoulders.

Epilogue

"All I am, all I ever hope to be, I owe to my angel mother."

—ABRAHAM LINCOLN,
speaking of Sarah Bush Lincoln,
his stepmother

Bibliography

BOOKS

Arnstein, Helene S. *What to Tell Your Child: About Birth, Illness, Death, Divorce, and Other Family Crises.* New York: Condor Publishing, 1978.

Atkin, Edith, and Estelle Rubin. *Part Time Father: A Guide for the Divorced Father.* New York: The Vanguard Press, 1976.

Baer, Jean. *The Second Wife.* Garden City, New York: Doubleday & Company, 1972.

Bohannan, Paul, ed. *Divorce and After.* Garden City, New York: Doubleday & Company, 1970.

Dodson, Fitzhugh. *How to Discipline—with Love.* New York: Rawson, Wade Publishers, 1977.

Duberman, Lucile. *The Reconstituted Family: A Study of Remarried Couples and Their Children.* Chicago, Illinois: Nelson-Hall, 1975.

Gardner, Richard A. *The Boys and Girls Book About Divorce.* New York: Bantam, 1977.

———. *The Parents' Book About Divorce.* Garden City, New York: Doubleday & Company, 1977.

———. *Psychotherapy With Children of Divorce.* New York: Jason Aronson, 1976.

Hayward, Brooke. *Haywire.* New York: Alfred A. Knopf, 1977.

LeShan, Eda. *What's Going to Happen to Me? When Parents Separate or Divorce.* New York: Four Winds Press, 1978.

Levine, James A. *Who Will Raise the Children? New Options for Fathers (and Mothers).* Philadelphia and New York: J. B. Lippincott, 1976.

Lowe, Patricia Tracy. *The Cruel Stepmother.* Englewood Cliffs, New Jersey: Prentice-Hall, Inc., 1970.

Maddox, Brenda. *The Half-Parent: Living With Other People's Children.* New York: The Vanguard Press, 1976.

Mayleas, Davidyne. *Rewedded Bliss.* New York: Basic Books, Inc., 1977.

Nadler, Janice Horowitz. *The Psychological Stress of the Stepmother.* A dissertation approved for the degree Doctor of Philosophy by the Faculty of the California School of Professional Psychology, Los Angeles, 1976.

Reingold, Carmel Berman. *Remarriage.* New York: Harper & Row, 1976.

Roosevelt, Ruth, and Jeanette Lofas. *Living in Step: A Remarriage Manual for Parents and Children.* New York: McGraw Hill Paperbacks, 1977.

Salk, Lee. *What Every Child Would Like Parents to Know About Divorce.* New York: Harper & Row, 1978.

Simon, Anne W. *Stepchild in the Family: A View of Children in Remarriage.* New York: The Odyssey Press, 1964.

Victor, Ira, and Win Ann Winkler. *Fathers and Custody.* New York: Hawthorn Books, 1977.

Westoff, Leslie Aldridge. *The Second Time Around: Remarriage in America.* New York: The Viking Press, 1977.

ARTICLES

Bohannan, Paul, and Rosemary Erickson. "Stepping In," *Psychology Today,* Jan. 1978.

Bowerman, Charles E., and Donald P. Irish. "Some Relationships of Stepchildren to Their Parents," *Marriage and Family Living,* May 1962.

Duberman, Lucile. "Step-Kin Relationships," *Journal of Marriage and the Family,* May 1973.

Dullea, Georgia. "Children Who Are Going to the Altar With the Parent Who Marries Again," *New York Times,* Jan. 3, 1978.

Flaste, Richard. "Family Life Poses Poignant Problems for the Stepparent," *New York Times,* April 18, 1977.

Glick, Paul C., and Arthur J. Norton. "Marrying, Divorcing, and Living Together in the U.S. Today," *Population Bulletin,* vol. 32, no. 5 (Population Reference Bureau, Inc. Washington, D.C., 1977).

Liddick, Betty. "The Frustrating Role of the Stepparent," *Los Angeles Times,* Nov. 27, 1977.

Marks, Judy. "The Cinderella Syndrome: Working Out Stepparent

Problems," *Teen*, vol. 22, no. 5, May 1978.

Pfleger, Janet. "The Wicked Stepmother in a Child Guidance Clinic," *Smith College Studies in Social Work*, vol. 17, no. 3, March 1947.

Salk, Lee. "You and Your Stepchildren," *Harper's Bazaar*, June 1975.

Schulman, Gerda L. "Myths That Intrude on the Adaptation of the Stepfamily," *Social Casework*, March 1972.

Stephen, Beverly. "The His and Hers Family," *Sunday News Magazine*, Aug. 14, 1977.

Visher, Emily B., and John S. Visher. "Common Problems of Stepparents and Their Spouses," *American Journal of Orthopsychiatry*, vol. 48, no. 2, April 1978.

Index